MULTI-TRACK DIPLOMACY BETWEEN INDIA AND PAKISTAN: A CONCEPTUAL FRAMEWORK FOR SUSTAINABLE SECURITY

The Regional Centre for Strategic Studies (RCSS) is an independent, non-profit and non-governmental organization for collaborative research, networking and interaction on strategic and international issues pertaining to South Asia. Set up in 1992, the RCSS is based in Colombo, Sri Lanka.

The RCSS is a South Asian forum for studies, training and multi-track dialogue and deliberation on issues of regional interest. All activities of RCSS are designed with a South Asia focus and are usually participated by experts from all South Asian countries. The Centre is envisaged as a forum for advancing the cause of co-operation, security, conflict resolution, confidence building, peace and development in the countries of the South Asian region.

The RCSS serves its South Asian and international constituency by: (a) networking programmes that promote interaction, communication and exchange between institutions and individuals within and outside the region engaged in South Asian strategic studies; (b) organizing regional workshops and seminars and sponsoring and coordinating collaborative research-, and (c) disseminating output of the research through publications which include books, monographs and a quarterly newsletter. The RCSS facilitates scholars and other professionals of South Asia to address, mutually and collectively, problems and, issues of topical interest for all countries of the region.

Queries may be addressed to:

Regional Centre for Strategic Studies
2 Elibank Road
Colombo 5
SRI LANKA
Tel: (94-11) 2599734, 599735
Fax: 2599993; e-mail: edrcss@sri.lanka.net
RCSS website: http://www.rcss.org

RCSS Policy Studies 30

Multi-Track Diplomacy between India and Pakistan: A Conceptual Framework for Sustainable Security

MANJRIKA SEWAK

REGIONAL CENTRE FOR STRATEGIC STUDIES
COLOMBO

MANOHAR
2005

Published by
Ajay Kumar Jain for
Manohar Publishers & Distributors
4753/23 Ansari Road, Daryaganj
New Delhi 110 002
and
Regional Centre for Strategic Studies
2 Elibank Road
Colombo 5
SRI LANKA
Tel: (94-11) 2599734-5; Fax: 2599993;
e-mail: edrcss@sri.lanka.net
Website: http://www.rcss.org

First published 2005

Views expressed in materials published in RCSS Policy Studies are of contributors, and not necessarily of the Regional Centre for Strategic Studies

ISBN 81-7304-621-2

Printed at
Lordson Publishers Pvt Ltd
Delhi 110 007

Distributed in South Asia by
FOUNDATION BOOKS
4381/4, Ansari Road
Daryaganj, New Delhi 110 002
and its branches at Mumbai, Hyderabad,
Bangalore, Chennai, Kolkata

Contents

RCSS is grateful to the
Nuclear Threat Initiative (NTI) for its generous
support for the RCSS-NTI Award
on which this report is based.

Acknowledgements

This study is the outcome of a research grant I received from the Regional Centre for Strategic Studies (RCSS) and the Nuclear Threat Initiative (NTI) in December 2003.

My appreciation is due to Prof. Sridhar Khatri and RCSS who provided me with the opportunity to undertake this study.

My mentor Dr Meenakshi Gopinath introduced me to the field of peacebuilding. I have learned so much from her. Her vision and unwavering commitment to conflict transformation and the peace process between Pakistan and India in particular, have been a great source of inspiration for this research.

My deep gratitude and thanks are due to Prof. Varun Sahni, my supervisor, without whose consistent guidance and encouragement this study would not have been possible. Prof. Sahni's incisive feedback and conceptual inputs have been of invaluable help.

I wish to thank all those who generously shared their time and expertise with me. Their perspectives have greatly enriched this publication.

In this study, I have drawn extensively from the teachings of the Conflict Transformation Programme (CTP) at the Eastern Mennonite University in Harrisonburg, Virginia. I acknowledge with deep appreciation the contributions of professors and colleagues at CTP whose writings have informed this study.

MANJRIKA SEWAK

Introduction

The idea for this research study was generated by a question often asked in contexts of protracted conflict: How are social change processes initiated? The complexity of such an inquiry is reflected in the plethora of questions it brings forth: What is social change? What kinds of values, relationships, capacities, roles and institutions would need to be developed and nurtured in order to achieve such change? Which actors, if brought together, would have the ability, because of their location and skills/expertise in a given setting, to initiate and sustain constructive change processes?

When applied to the relationship between India and Pakistan, these questions point to the realisation that the ending or resolution of conflict is not sufficient for social change. They compel us to ask more questions: What is it that we are trying to build? What kinds of relationships, institutions and cultures are we trying to create and nurture? This, in turn, brings forth the awareness that while the 'what' or the content of a conflict is important, social change happens only when the 'what' is held in relationship with the 'how' (strategies, methodologies and processes) and the ‘[illegible] (the actors who when brought together to work collectively have the capacity to sustain change) in a conflict setting.[1]

This study introduces the concept of sustainable peace and security as the vision, which informs the contours of social change processes between India and Pakistan. The process and methodology of multi-track diplomacy is introduced as a conceptual framework

[1] This perspective is drawn from the writings of sociologist and conflict transformation scholar John Paul Lederach who has worked in support of conciliation processes in regions of conflict such as Northern Ireland, Nicaragua and Tajikistan.

through which the goal of sustainable peace and security can be achieved between the two countries.

This thesis has been developed following an analysis of the conflict between Pakistan and India, which can be described as *protracted* (because it has continued for a long period of time), *intractable* (because it has been resistant to sustainable positive change for more than fifty years), and *deep-rooted* (because it has affected the thinking and attitudes of people in different sections of society in the two countries; the hostility has not been limited to governments, but rather has permeated into public discourse). At the heart of such conflicts lies the notion of perception. This includes perceptions about the conflict as well as the enemy. Such perceptions are partially based on objective facts and figures. The more important ingredients are subjective, particularly the emotions of fear, suspicion, anger and prejudice.

The challenge presented by a conflict such as this (and many other contemporary conflicts with similar characteristics) requires a radical shift in our thinking about conflict and its resolution, and how sustainable security can be built. What it requires most is a willingness to acknowledge that protracted, intractable and deep-rooted conflicts need the energy and expertise of a range of stakeholders—governmental and non-governmental. These include, in addition to government diplomats and the political and military leadership, actors from a cross-section of civil society (NGOs, educators, journalists, lawyers, trauma counsellors, community organisers, women's groups, business leaders and religious leaders). Commenting on the protracted and deep-rooted nature of contemporary conflicts, conflict resolution scholar Kevin Clements notes that such conflicts compel 'state systems to acknowledge that their power and legitimacy rest on the willing rather than the enforced compliance of citizens and that they exist to satisfy the needs and to promote the interests of their citizens rather than the interests and needs of the state system.'[2]

In this context, sustainable peace and security connote much more than the announcement of a ceasefire or the implementation

[2] Kevin Clements, 'Civil Society and Conflict Prevention', *Facing Ethnic Conflicts* (Bonn: Centre for Development Research, 14-16 December 2000), p. 2.

of a negotiated settlement. To begin with, they require the initiation of conciliation (and reconciliation) processes between hostile nations. As Richard Solomon, President of the United States Institute of Peace, Washington DC notes: 'Sustainable peace requires that long-time antagonists not merely lay down their arms, but that they achieve profound reconciliation that will endure because it is sustained by a society-wide network of relationships and mechanisms that promote justice and address the root causes of enmity before they can regenerate destabilising tensions.'[3] 'This amounts to a "paradigmatic shift" away from the traditional framework and activities that make up statist diplomacy—"away from a concern with the resolution of issues and toward a frame of reference that provides a focus on the restoration and rebuilding of relationships".'[4]

Multi-track diplomacy—introduced here as a process and methodology for sustainable peace and security—refers to a complex web of approaches, roles, strategies and activities employed by diverse actors at different stages of conflict development, conflict resolution and post-conflict peacebuilding. It includes the entire range of processes from crisis management and negotiation to the more long-term efforts at conciliation, transformative dialogue, relationship building, peace education, non-violence training, and restorative processes for justice and reconciliation. It extends beyond the achievement of a ceasefire and includes a range of actors including government diplomats, politicians, conflict resolution professionals, women's groups, community leaders, non-violence trainers, journalists, NGO workers, academics, business leaders, trauma healers and justice advocates. An important leitmotif in a multi-track framework is the focus on a plurality of approaches and actors to build sustainable security. The assumption is that there are several unique ways to help conflictants find common ground and citizens can use their own 'vocation and location' within a society to promote peace and security.

[3] Richard Solomon, 'Foreword', in John Paul Lederach, *Building Peace: Sustainable Reconciliation in Divided Societies* (Washington DC: United States Institute of Peace, 1997), p. ix.

The arguments put forth in this study are informed by the growing belief, among conflict resolution professionals, that while there are some things that only governments can do, there are others that only human beings outside government can do. Parallel to the official track, peace and security need to be built at the level of conflictual relationships, at the root of conflict, and not simply at the level of symptoms. In other words, sustainable peace and security can be built only if the energies, perspectives and experiences of all the stakeholders, particularly those at the grassroots—who experience conflict at an intimate level—are injected into official peace processes.

In this study, Chapter One begins by exploring the following questions: What is it that we are trying to build? What is the vision of social change that India and Pakistan envisage, or ought to envisage? This chapter introduces the notion of sustainable security as the vision that India and Pakistan should strive to achieve in the coming years. It is seen as the goal that informs the contours of social change processes between the two countries. In envisioning sustainable security, this study draws on insights from diverse areas and fields such as peace and conflict studies, feminist scholarship in international relations, and contemporary writings on human security.

Chapter Two introduces the concept of track two diplomacy as professional, non-governmental action that has the capacity (and motivation) to strengthen and support governments in their efforts to prevent and resolve intrastate and interstate conflicts. The potential role of track two diplomacy as a bridge between governments and civil society groups is also explored here. In addition, a comparative study of the evolution of non-official dialogue processes between the United States and the former Soviet Union is conducted in order to extract the *best practices* and *lessons learned* that might be insightful for track two processes between Pakistan and India.

Chapter Three broadens the discussion on non-governmental peacebuilding by introducing multi-track diplomacy as an integrated framework through which the goal of sustainable peace and security, between India and Pakistan, can be achieved. It traces the evolution, philosophy and methodology of multi-track diplomacy, at a conceptual and practical level. Currently, there exists a considerable amount of conceptual fuzziness about the terminology of multi-track diplomacy, which has been used to refer to very different civil society processes in various regions of conflict. This is primarily because there exist significant points of departure in terms of how multi-track actors (their goals and functions) have been defined in South Asia and in North America and Europe. Special attention is, therefore, given to the conceptual understanding of this term and its application in the context of the peace process between Pakistan and India.

Drawing on the work of conflict transformation scholar John Paul Lederach, Chapter Four shifts the focus of discussion to longer-term timeframes by addressing the complex challenge of *sustaining* social change. In other words, once peace and security have been achieved, what mechanism does a multi-track framework offer for sustaining such broad-based change? In this chapter, the foci and levels of intervention (by governmental and non-governmental tracks) are linked with the different timeframes in which they occur. In addition to providing a unique set of lenses to examine the factors that sustain the India-Pakistan conflict, such a web brings forth the important roles that the civil society tracks can play in building long-term peace and security.

Chapter Five presents a critical evaluation of the multi-track framework. In addition to highlighting the contributions and successes of multi-track diplomacy, it draws attention to the challenges that confront those working in this field, and how these might be addressed. This chapter also highlights the specific contributions of multi-track initiatives to the peace process between India and Pakistan, and makes recommendations for strengthening their role, efficacy and impact in the long run.

The concluding chapter—*From Intractability to Sustainability*—returns to the central questions of this study: How can constructive social change processes be initiated and sustained between Pakistan and India? How might the vision of sustainable security inform these processes? What role can multi-track diplomacy play in building long-term peace and security between the two countries? Lifting out the connections between these questions, this chapter foregrounds the key concepts on which the thesis of this study rests: *relationship*, *process*, *capacity*, *coordination*, *collaboration*, *inclusivity*, *diversity* and *transformation*.

CHAPTER ONE

Visioning Sustainable Security

> The world we have made, as a result of the level of thinking we have done thus far, creates problems we cannot solve at the same level of thinking at which we created them.
>
> ALBERT EINSTEIN

This study argues that the concept of security should be broadened to a more comprehensive notion of sustainable security, which facilitates the integration of multi-disciplinary perspectives. In exploring the contours of sustainable security, it draws on insights from peace and conflict studies' research, feminist scholarship on security and writings on human security.

In the years since the end of the Cold War, security studies has broadened beyond its traditional focus, which included the study of war, deterrence, military force and arms races. The field of peace and conflict studies, which emerged in the 1960s (and gained momentum through the initiation of academic programmes in universities in the 1980s), seeks to broaden the concept of security to include social and economic factors and to make it multi-dimensional and multi-level.

The field of peace and conflict studies (because of its inter-disciplinary origins—political science, psychology, religion, physics and sociology) tends to be more wide-ranging in the issues it considers worthy of attention in the study of security affairs. It connects war and peace with individual responsibility, economic equality, gender relations, cross-cultural understanding, and other aspects of social relationships. It seeks the potential for peace not only in the transactions of state leaders but also in the transformation of entire societies.[1]

In fleshing out the concept of sustainable security, this chapter borrows heavily from this field because it moves significantly beyond describing the world as it is, to exploring how it should or could be, and then suggests approaches and models for getting there. This chapter also draws on feminist scholarship in international relations, which has contributed significantly to expanding the margins of the security discourse by foregrounding values and principles that have been shunned by traditional approaches to security.

SUSTAINABILITY: GENERATIONAL VISIONING

Sustainability can be defined as our ability to 'meet the needs of the present generation without compromising the ability of future generations to meet their own needs'.[2] What need to be sustained are life support systems and the ability of individuals, groups and nations to reach their fullest potential.

The notion of sustainability compels us to think long-term and take a 'generational approach' to issues of peace and security. It calls for generational visioning where policies and discourses are informed by a vision of what governments and civil society would want to see realised after twenty years. It compels us to ask ourselves: What kind of security environment would we want to leave for the next generation? Are our current policies and actions enhancing the security of future generations of Indians and Pakistanis? For how long can Pakistan and India sustain a deterrence relationship, particularly nuclear deterrence? Can the two countries afford to sustain this conflict for another half-century?

An attempt to meld the notion of sustainability with security points us in the direction of a setting where present and future generations of decision-makers and civil society leaders would have

[1] Johan Galtung, *Peace by Peaceful Means: Peace and Conflict, Development and Civilization* (Thousand Oaks, California: Sage, 1996).

[2] The World Commission on Environment and Development (1987) cited in the *Encyclopaedia of Sustainable Development* www.doc.mmu.ac.uk/aric/esd/menu.html

the motivation, expertise and skills to prevent and transform protracted conflicts by choosing dialogue and coexistence over the use (or threat of use) of force and violence. Such a 'generational approach to security' is crucial if it is to be sustainable.

An important element of sustainability, therefore, relates to the ability of human beings and states to take actions that address immediate security needs while focusing on long-term goals. It involves a process where states explore options for responding in the present in ways that respect the past, while being guided by the possibilities and hopes for the future. Such long-term visioning has the potential to facilitate a holistic understanding of security because it compels human beings to visualise a world that they would want to leave for their children and grandchildren.

The notion of sustainability is closely linked with visioning processes. For instance, to arrive at a sustainable understanding of security, Pakistan and India need to conceptualise a vision that they might want to see realised after a decade or two. Write Sanjeev Khagram, William Clark and Dana Raad: 'The genius of sustainability lies in its ability to provide "space" for serious attempts to grapple with the real, dynamic and complex relationships among societies, economies and natural environments, as well as between past, present and the future.'[3]

VISIONING SUSTAINABLE SECURITY

Barry Buzan, Professor of International Relations at the London School of Economics, answers the question of what makes something a security issue by positing that security is about survival. When an issue is represented as posing an existential threat to a designated referent object (traditionally but not necessarily the state), it becomes a security issue.[4] Drawing on Arnold Wolfers' discussion of security as 'the absence of threat to acquired values',

[3] Sanjeev Khagram, William Clark and Dana Firas Raad, 'From the Environment and Human Security to Sustainable Security and Development', *Journal of Human Development*, Vol. 4, No. 2, (Cambridge, MA: Carfax Publishing, July 2003), p. 296.

[4] Barry Buzan, Ole Waever, Jaap de Wilde, *Security: A New Framework for Analysis* (Boulder, Colorado: Lynne Rienner Publishers, 1998), p. 21.

David Baldwin defines security as 'a low probability of damage to acquired values'.[5]

Since the end of the Cold War, the contours of the discourse on security—which traditionally has been informed on the basis of how states use force to manage threats to their territorial integrity and domestic political order—have changed significantly, with a growing awareness that security is not restricted to the territorial integrity or well-being of the state.

Commenting on the growing untenability of traditional formulations of security, Harold Saunders, former US Assistant Secretary of State for Near Eastern and South Asian Affairs, writes: 'In the past, nation-states were perceived as rational institutions in which leaders amassed power to pursue objectively defined interests in a strategic chess game with another state. In that image, states resolve problems by the use or threat of military or economic power and by formal negotiation. Today, unilateral action seems less and less effective.'[6]

Harold Saunders introduces three realities to validate this argument. First, in a nuclear world, the security of one state depends on the others' sense of security. This is particularly true of India and Pakistan where each derives its sense of security from how secure the other makes it feel. Neither can be secure unless the two cooperate. A sustainable security formulation needs to be based on an understanding that security for ones' own people is dependent on how secure those who are seen as *the other* feel.[7]

[5] David Baldwin, 'The Concept of Security', *Review of International Studies,* Vol. 23 (1997) cited in Kanti Bajpai, 'Human Security: Concept and Measurement', *Kroc Institute Occasional Paper #19: OP: 1* (August 2000), p. 13.

[6] Harold Saunders, *The Other Walls: The Arab-Israeli Peace Process in a Global Perspective* (Princeton, NJ: Princeton University Press, 1985), pp. 149-50.

Following his retirement from the US government as Assistant Secretary of State for Near Eastern and South Asian Affairs, Harold Saunders joined the Kettering Foundation and recently launched the International Institute for Sustained Dialogue to conduct research on the methodology of citizens' diplomacy and its application in different social and political contexts.

[7] This understanding is prevalent in several indigenous cultures, most prominently in Africa, where the term *obuntu* (I am because you are) connotes an acknowledgement of the interdependent nature of the human community.

This point can also be used to argue that rather than amassing military power, the building of a web of concrete relationships between people and institutions in the two countries, will lead to sustainable security.

Second, there is a 'broadening participation of people, both in the governance of nations and in the relationships between nations. Focusing on the political energies and interaction of communities of people—not just on state institutions—compels us to think in different ways about the causes and resolution of conflict. . . . The revolution in communication, transportation and information has enabled more and more citizens to harness their own political power in new ways to tackle protracted conflicts. To accomplish this, they are thinking about politics in creative, non-institutional ways. . . . They are asking whether governments are capable of providing security and building peace.'[8]

'As the role of people increases, interaction between public agendas in civil societies plays a larger part in relationships between nations. Those agendas reflect the "gut reactions" of the citizens of one nation to the perceived character and intent of other nations.' Saunders thus questions the proposition that states are to be analysed as institutions quite different from the groups of human beings who influence, make, implement and sustain their policies.

Third, traditional instruments of statecraft (such as the exercise of various forms of military or economic power, or as a non-violent alternative, negotiation) often do not reliably accomplish what is expected of them. In a nuclear context, sanctions and the threat or the exercise of military power are certainly dangerous options. Adds Saunders: 'Focusing primarily on states amassing military and economic power to pursue objectively defined interests in competition with other states does not provide an adequate

---

Although *obuntu* has traditionally been used among communities and groups, it is extremely relevant in the context of the conflict between Pakistan and India. This is because there is no escaping the fact that the futures of succeeding generations of Pakistanis and Indians are inextricably linked and that it is the responsibility of the current generation to find ways to actively coexist.

[8] Harold Saunders, *The Other Walls: The Arab-Israeli Peace Process in a Global Perspective* (Princeton, NJ: Princeton University Press, 1985), pp. 150-51.

conception of relations among nations today. Relations among nations are increasingly a continuous political process of complex interaction between significant elements of whole bodies politic. This interaction includes but reaches beyond policy-making and policy-influencing communities on both sides of a relationship. As civil societies develop and people increasingly influence and participate in cross-border relationships, change often takes place through that interaction at many levels at once rather than mainly through a linear series of government actions and responses. Looking beyond the power and policy-making of individual governments acting on one another, we begin to see the total pattern of interaction—the overall relationship—between whole bodies politic.'[9]

This presents a more nuanced understanding of the ways in which the changing nature and complexities of contemporary conflicts and relations between states impact formulations of security. It compels us to expand our understanding of security from a focus solely on the territorial integrity of states. This leads to the question: How might we find the balance between investing in people and meeting threats to territorial integrity? This dilemma is most visibly reflected in literature that juxtaposes the 'benefits of peace' with the 'costs of war' between India and Pakistan. While the military manpower of India and Pakistan are the fourth and seventh largest in the world respectively, according to the Human Development Report (2003) of the United Nations Development Programme, out of 191 countries, they rank 127 and 144 in terms of human development. In India, close to 500 million people barely manage to survive and subsist, while the benefits of planned development accrue to less than a third of the population. Pakistan incurs an equal amount of expenditure on military and development (3.8 per cent of GDP), while India spends 2.7 per cent of GDP on military and 6.2 per cent on development. If troops are mobilised again (on the pattern of the mobilisation in 2002), it will cost India 0.46 per cent of GDP and Pakistan 2.25 per cent of GDP.[10]

[9] Ibid., p. 154.

[10] In February 2004, the Strategic Foresight Group came out with a report

Although the traditional understanding of security has changed significantly over the last decade, the growing interdependence of states (particularly in economic relations), and the threats of nuclear annihilation and environmental degradation suggest that a 'statist approach' to national security may soon become unsustainable. This is particularly true in the context of Pakistan and India where the economic benefits of cooperation point to the potential for an interdependent and prosperous future. Mutual understanding and trust become particularly crucial in this context. Such trust must rest on a realisation that the nuclear status of India and Pakistan and their growing interdependence in a globalising world makes the notion of zero-sum games and win-lose solutions dysfunctional.

It is in this context that multi-track diplomacy, which offers diverse approaches and methodologies, assumes significance. Civil society initiatives that engage in cross-border multi-track processes have the potential to build trust and respect between the two countries and also create a constituency that supports greater interaction and interdependence.

This study draws substantially from the human security paradigm to explore the contours of a sustainable understanding of security. According to Kanti Bajpai, 'human security relates to the protection of the individual's personal safety and freedom from direct and indirect threats of violence. The promotion of human development and good governance, and when necessary, the collective use of sanctions and force are central to managing human security.... States, international organisations, non-governmental organisations and other groups in civil society, in combination, are vital to the prospects of human security.'[11] This, according to Bajpai, brings to the fore several vital questions, some of which are: 'security for

titled *Cost of Conflict between India and Pakistan*, which lists the human, economic, socio-political, and diplomatic costs of the conflict. Major General (Retd.) Mahmud Ali Durrani also presents a detailed analysis of the impact of heavy defence expenditure on governance patterns, economic backwardness and human development in his book *India and Pakistan: The Costs of Conflict and The Benefits of Peace* (Karachi: Oxford University Press, 2001).

[11] Kanti Bajpai, 'Human Security: Concept and Measurement', *Kroc Institute Occasional Paper #19: OP: 1* (August 2000), p. 48.

whom, security of which values, security from what threats, and security by what means'.[12]

A formulation of security, which places the individual as the referent, broadens the security agenda. A sustainable notion of security would, therefore, imply the survival and dignity of human beings through 'freedom from fear' and 'freedom from want'. It would hold the 'protection and welfare of human beings' as central to any understanding of security. As the late Mahbub ul Haq put it: 'We need to fashion a new concept of security that is reflected in the lives of our people, not in the weapons of our country.'[13]

This is not to suggest that the security of individuals should be pursued at the expense of territorial integrity, but rather that the balance between state sovereignty and peoples' sense of security be redressed. As Kanti Bajpai puts it: 'Human security does not ignore state security, but it treats it as no more than co-equal to individual security. . . . The state is the provider of security for the citizenry; it is a *means* to security, and its security cannot be the *end* of security.'[14] As Lloyd Axworthy, the former Foreign Minister of Canada notes: 'Traditional security concerns remain important, but they are not sufficient for stability and peace.'[15]

The basic human needs theory, propounded by John Burton, posits the existence of certain universal needs that must be satisfied if people are to feel secure and if protracted conflicts are to be transformed.[16] All human beings are seen as possessing a set of non-negotiable needs—material (food, shelter, health care and employment—'freedom from want'), cultural (right to religion,

[12] David Baldwin, 'The Concept of Security', *Review of International Studies*, Vol. 23 (1997) cited in Kanti Bajpai, 'Human Security: Concept and Measurement', *Kroc Institute Occasional Paper #19: OP: 1* (August 2000), p. 14.

[13] Mahbub ul Haq, 'New Imperatives of Human Security', *RGICS Paper No. 17*, Rajiv Gandhi Institute for Contemporary Studies (New Delhi: Rajiv Gandhi Foundation, 1994), p. 1.

[14] Kanti Bajpai, 'Human Security: Concept and Measurement', *Kroc Institute Occasional Paper #19: OP: 1* (August 2000), p. 37.

[15] Ibid., p. 22.

[16] John Burton has made a significant contribution to the emerging study of basic human needs in his book *Conflict: Human Needs Theory* (Wellington, New Zealand: Macmillan Press Ltd, 1993).

language) and social needs (respect, dignity and 'freedom from fear'). The need for life to be perceived as being predictable and safe is extremely important in this context. If these needs are not met in socially accepted ways, individuals/groups begin to feel insecure, and this insecurity perpetuates conflict.

The basic human needs for identity and security are particularly important in the context of Pakistan and India. While the positions taken by the two countries (on Kashmir, cross-border terrorism, etc.) might seem incompatible, if one were to scratch the surface and dig deeper to identify the basic human needs, one would find a great deal of similarity. The actions of both countries are guided by a need for security, identity and existence (particularly for Pakistanis, many of whom still believe that Indians have not accepted their birth and national identity).[17] Perhaps, the greatest source of insecurity is the profound lack of contact between the two polities. Such sources of insecurity can be transformed through vibrant civil society engagement and multi-track diplomacy, which emphasises recognition, mutual respect, reconciliation and co-existence. What is important here is that while private citizens and civil society groups in the two countries should build on their commonalities, they also need to recognise and respect the differences that exist between their identities (rather than attempt to remove these differences).

In such a formulation, a reliance on arms for security, the proliferation of weapons of mass destruction and structural violence can emerge as threats to security. Peace and conflict studies' scholar, Johan Galtung, conceptualises the notion of 'threats to security' in terms of violence, which is direct/visible as also that which is structural/indirect. 'Violence is present when the actual somatic and mental realisations of human beings are below their potential

[17] Beena Sarwar, a journalist based in Karachi, notes that 'there is a widely held perception in Pakistan that India has never accepted its existence and is always working to destroy it, economically and physically—a perception that the establishment (in Pakistan) has encouraged'. 'Women's Role in Building Peace between India and Pakistan' (Montreal: Centre for Research and Teaching on Women, McGill University, 30 July-1 August 2004), p. 2 www.mcgill.ca/mcrtw/peace/resources

realisations.'[18] Violence of this kind may be found in legal structures, political bodies, governance institutions, repressive trade agreements, arms races, etc. Such violence is more of a process than an event, and is therefore complex and protracted. The proliferation of small arms and weapons of mass destruction and interstate war can become significant sources of structural violence.

Threats can, therefore, be seen as direct as well as indirect, emanating from state and non-state actors and also from structural sources.[19] How might, for instance, tensions, crises and even war, affect human security? Kanti Bajpai points out that the expectation of and preparation for war can have social effects with consequences for individual safety. These effects can be encapsulated in the term militarism, which may be defined as 'the propagation and privileging of symbols, values and practices associated with organised violence'.[20] In this context, militarism, which permeates social and political life, emerges as an important source of structural violence. Writes Bajpai: 'The fear of civil or state violence can leave individuals in thrall as much as the actual application of violence. The symbolic and demonstrative effect of police and paramilitary forces as a deterrent or as a coercive inducement is enough to make people behave in ways that they may not otherwise wish.'[21] Protracted conflicts such as the India-Pakistan imbroglio therefore become dangerous sources of human insecurity.

This brings us to the moot question of the means through which sustainable security can be achieved. The human security paradigm places emphasis on human development, grassroots participation, a reduction in arms expenditures and the provision of a context for the flourishing of a free, broad-based civil society. 'The threat or the use of force is seen as an instrument, but to be used as a last resort and in partnership with other countries. Various

[18] Kathleen Maas Weigert, 'Structural Violence', in *Encyclopaedia of Violence, Peace and Conflict*, Vol. 3 (New York: Academic Press, 1999), p. 432.

[19] Meenakshi Gopinath, 'Trenches, Boundaries and Spaces: The Dialectics of Governance and Security in India', in P.R. Chari (ed.), *Security and Governance in South Asia* (New Delhi: Manohar, 2001), p. 53.

[20] Kanti Bajpai, 'Human Security: Concept and Measurement', *Kroc Institute Occasional Paper #19: OP: 1* (August 2000), p. 43.

[21] Ibid., p. 29.

kinds of sanctions are preferred over force. Long-term cooperation is seen as necessary, particularly since the world is increasingly interdependent and states are more porous than ever.'[22]

Therefore, through the lens of sustainable security, humane governance, sustainable development, gender equality, human rights and social equity become as important to regional and global peace as arms control and disarmament.

The human security paradigm has been challenged on various grounds. First, it has been said that it loses its theoretical utility by identifying such a broad range of factors as threats to security; second, by including a range of factors relating to structural violence, there is little hope of framing a coherent policy response. However, this critique reflects an important shortcoming of the realist lens, which is its failure to address the growing complexity of contemporary security threats.

In today's world, security can no longer be limited to the simplistic understanding that interstate war is the most significant threat to individuals and communities and that the use of force (or the threat of it) is the most effective strategy for preventing war or armed conflict. What is needed is a security paradigm that recognises the importance of expecting, accepting and working with complexities rather than using complex situations and issues to block peace processes or unrealistically attempting to remove complexities altogether. As Kanti Bajpai notes: 'It cannot be the case that confronted by a complex and dangerous world that confounds our theoretical and policy "comfort zones", we climb back into those zones.'[23]

The growing literature on 'non-traditional formulations of security points to the need to refrain from seeing non-military variables as forming part of an alternative discourse, but rather as a nuanced, refining input to arrive at an expanded, holistic and inclusive notion of what must constitute security concerns of nation states.'[24]

22 Ibid., p. 30.

23 Ibid., p. 51.

24 Sumona DasGupta, 'Concept Note for Regional Conference on Non-Traditional Security Discourse: Gender and South Asia' (New Delhi: WISCOMP, December 2003).

A non-traditional formulation of security questions the priority given to military security and considers economic, social and political stability as the real source of security and the adoption of a conflict resolution approach as one that can yield sustainable peace and security. In fact, according to Moonis Ahmar, Professor of International Relations, University of Karachi, Pakistan, the upsurge of extremist ethnic and religious groups in South Asia provides empirical evidence that a military-centred approach to security is not working—an approach, which he sees as the cause of such growing fundamentalism. He notes that in a non-traditional security paradigm, forces of intolerance generally do not assert themselves because the democratic and decentralised political order is not supportive of their role.[25] This is an important point because a strong culture of coexistence and pluralism that can combat the forces of religious fanaticism is integral to the notion of sustainable security.

MILITARY SECURITY THROUGH THE LENS OF SUSTAINABILITY

All these arguments lead to the question: Can military security lead to sustainable security? According to Rajesh Basrur, military security relates to the security of life of the national community from external threats—nuclear or conventional.[26] The theoretical underpinnings of the overwhelming reliance on military security are informed by the theory of realism, which focuses on the interaction between sovereign states in the pursuit of competitive national interests, posited on power. Realism privileges the state while simultaneously ignoring social structures, peoples' movements, marginalised groups and non-state actors.[27] In this context, 'the

[25] Moonis Ahmar, 'South Asian Security in the New Millennium', in Rajesh Basrur (ed.), *Security in the New Millennium: Views from South Asia* (New Delhi: India Research Press, 2001), p. 205.

[26] Rajesh Basrur (ed.), *Security in the New Millennium: Views from South Asia* (New Delhi: India Research Press, 2001), p. 173.

[27] Anuradha Chenoy, 'Militarisation, Conflict and Women in South Asia', in Lois Lorentzen, Jennifer Turpin (eds), *The Women and War Reader* (New York: New York University Press, 1998).

human security discourse has come up from below, from peoples and groups excluded from the national security debate, defined and articulated by civil society groups, social movements and marginal groups, especially women.'[28]

This chapter questions the willingness to treat nuclear weapons as another instrument of state military power. It asks the question: Can Pakistan and India feel more secure through the traditional means of stockpiling weapons (conventional and nuclear) and threats of use of force? Can the two countries explore ways of preventing armed conflict, which go beyond deterrence? Efforts towards the 'idealistic goal' of nuclear disarmament, beginning with arms' control agreements, must be an important element of a sustainable security framework. In the context of Pakistan and India, there are good reasons to doubt that the Pokhran and Chagai nuclear tests have better served the goals of security. The Kargil conflict following these nuclear blasts represents the first major military confrontation between India and Pakistan in nearly 30 years, and demonstrates the fallacy that the likelihood of conventional war is reduced by nuclearisation of the two countries.[29] That nuclearisation would allow expenditure on conventional forces to be reduced was based on a thesis that nuclear deterrence subsumes conventional deterrence. This has given way to an acknowledgement in the Indian Draft Nuclear Doctrine that 'highly effective conventional military capabilities shall be maintained to raise the threshold of outbreak both of conventional military conflict as well as that of threat or use of nuclear weapons'.[30] The non-transparency of the nuclear chain of command and control, when linked to the limited knowledge that politicians have about what it means to own nuclear weapons contributes to a greater sense of insecurity.[31]

[28] Rita Manchanda, 'Redefining and Feminising Security', *Economic and Political Weekly*, Vol. 36, No. 22 (Mumbai, 2 June 2001), p. 1956.

[29] Amartya Sen, 'India and the Bomb', *Frontline*, Vol. 17, No. 19 (Chennai: 16–29 September 2000).

[30] P.R. Chari and Ayesha Siddiqe, 'Defence Expenditure in South Asia: India, Pakistan and Colombo', *RCSS Policy Studies 12* (Colombo: Regional Centre for Strategic Studies, 2000), pp. 10-11.

[31] A considerable amount of literature has emerged on this subject over the

The pertinent question is this: 'Will a limited conflict remain limited especially when it is fought under a nuclear shadow?' With the fragile communication system between India and Pakistan, is the concept of deterrence likely to work? The absence of an early warning system compounds the danger due to the proximity of the two countries.[32] The short flight time (less than 300 seconds) for a ballistic missile flight between India and Pakistan has grave implications for the feasibility and utility of an early warning system. There are also the problems of false alarms, which may automatically trigger an accidental nuclear war.

This study makes the argument that nuclear weapons have not enhanced the security of India and Pakistan. While a moratorium on nuclear tests, the installation of early warning systems, military CBMs, etc., are very important components of a sustainable security framework (given that nuclear weapons are a reality today and Pakistan and India are nowhere close to disarmament), such measures cannot in themselves sustain a sense of security. For this, one needs to delve into the layers of perceptions, misperceptions, and attitudes that compel countries to go nuclear in the first place. This means looking at the perceptions (including negative stereotypes and prejudices) of decision-makers and actors from a cross-section of civil society.[33]

If looked at through the lens of sustainability (where our actions are guided by the well-being of succeeding generations), the 'idealistic goal' of nuclear disarmament might not be so idealistic. Therefore, a sustainable security formulation would urge civil society and governments to conceptualise a long-term vision for change, which is responsive to the immediate and intermediate

---

last six years. The most recent and comprehensive writing on the subject is the book *Prisoners of the Nuclear Dream*, which is a collection of essays by Pakistanis and Indians, Ramana and Reddy (eds), Orient Longman, 2003.

[32] Comments made by Pervez Iqbal Cheema at the RCSS Summer Workshop on *Defence, Technology and Co-operative Security*, Shanghai, 2003.

[33] Robert Jervis, Professor of International Politics at Columbia University, has written extensively on this subject. Some of his publications on this topic include *Hypotheses on Misperception* (World Politics, 1968), and *Perception and Misperception in International Politics* (Princeton University Press, 1976).

needs for security. This would help framing approaches that are constructive, inclusive and visionary.

Such a conception of security compels us to look beyond realpolitik and statist approaches in search of models that enable citizens to visualise the kind of societies they would want to leave for the coming generations. In this context, civil society engagement across the different tracks and levels of peacebuilding is absolutely crucial.

'ENGENDERING' THE DISCOURSE ON PEACE AND SECURITY

In the realm of security, women's groups have advocated a broadening of the definition of security from one confined to territorial and military security to that which considers issues of individual dignity, social justice, gender equity, water security, food security, humane governance and environmental security as central to the shaping of international security—concerns that were earlier seen as 'soft issues'. In so doing, they have interrogated the militarist models of state security that have hitherto guided the mandate of government-led negotiations. For instance, several women's groups in Pakistan and India, assert the need to move beyond a peace that involves the mere absence of military conflict and arms races. They urge for a paradigm that foregrounds inclusive and mutually beneficial processes for dealing with the conflict.[34]

Feminist scholarship holds that the modern notion of human security has evolved from the comprehensive approach adopted by peace researchers, especially those who identify themselves as feminist peace researchers. Writes feminist peace researcher Betty Reardon: 'Women's peace groups were among the first to argue that real human security lies in the expectation of well-being that is found in protection against harm of all kinds, of the meeting of basic needs, of the experience of human dignity and the fulfilment

[34] Indian and Pakistani groups such as WIPSA (Women's Initiative for Peace in South Asia), ASR Resource Centre, Women's Action Forum and WISCOMP (Women in Security, Conflict Management and Peace) have been at the forefront of exploring broader understandings of peace and security.

of human rights and a healthy natural environment capable of sustaining life.'[35] 'Because women make up a disproportionate share of the economically disadvantaged, they are likely to have a more nuanced understanding of the implications of a militaristic foreign policy. They are likely to view high military expenditure as a drain on resources available for domestic social programmes.'[36] In the case of Pakistan and India, this is particularly true with women initiating cross-border contact not simply to talk about peace, but to also address issues of common concern such as social justice, violence against women (public and private), pluralism and participatory democracy.

Recognising the role that women's groups can play in building sustainable peace and security, in October 2000, the United Nations Security Council passed Resolution 1325, which calls for the participation of women in peace and security initiatives; the integration of gender perspectives in peacebuilding; and the protection of women (who are especially vulnerable) in regions of armed conflict. This Resolution acknowledges that women and children account for the vast majority of those adversely affected by conflict.

Feminist scholars such as Ann Tickner argue that traditional notions of national security, with their heavy emphasis on militarily defined security, do not ensure, and sometimes may even decrease, the security of individuals. They point to the inadequacy of realist models of international relations, built on assumptions of rigid boundary distinctions between outside and inside, anarchy and order, and foreign and domestic. These boundary distinctions fall short of providing frameworks for understanding the roots of conflict and for suggesting inclusive ways of thinking about security.[37]

[35] Betty Reardon, 'Women or Weapons: The Militarist Sexist Symbiosis', in Ingeborg Breines et al. (eds), *Towards a Women's Agenda for a Culture of Peace* (Paris: UNESCO Publishing, 1999).

[36] Rita Manchanda, 'Redefining and Feminising Security', *Economic and Political Weekly*, Vol. 36, No. 22 (Mumbai, 2 June 2001), p. 1956.

[37] J. Ann Tickner, *Gender in International Relations: Feminist Perspectives on Achieving Global Security* (New York: Columbia University Press, 1992), p. 133.

Feminist perspectives see traditional formulations of security as being strongly influenced by a 'hegemonic masculinity', which privileges characteristics such as 'autonomy, power, independence, and an instrumental notion of rationality'—characteristics that are 'not traditionally female'. 'A militarised version of security privileges masculine characteristics and elevates men to the status of first-class citizens by virtue of their role as providers of security.'[38] Through its questioning of realism, its critique of war, and its emphasis on the links between patriarchy, militarism and violence, feminist scholarship provides valuable insight into the notion of sustainable security.

A discourse that foregrounds the equally valued experiences of women and men contributes to processes of coexistence, diversity and inclusivity. In this context, important lessons can be learned from the Scandinavian countries. For example, in Norway, women occupy half the cabinet positions and there is a strong emphasis on what might be defined as 'non-traditional' concerns (health care, education, basic human needs). According to Ann Tickner, this suggests that states with less militaristic foreign policies and a greater commitment to socio-economic and ecological security may also rely on less gendered models of security. It is pertinent to note here that Norway, as a member of NATO, does not neglect military security. This defies the misplaced assumption that military security precludes human security. Although the Scandinavian countries do not confront security threats of the nature or magnitude that India and Pakistan do, this example nevertheless provides useful insight into the ways in which issues relating to gender, security, development and conflict coalesce and are framed, analysed and addressed.

Drawing on feminist scholarship, this study argues that genuine security requires not only the absence of war but also the elimination of unjust social and economic relations, and unequal gender relations. A sustainable notion of security would be one that privileges the values of 'attachment' and 'community'—values that have traditionally been excluded from the conception of

[38] Ibid., p. 128.

security. This is not to suggest that 'power' and 'autonomy', seen traditionally as masculine values, be replaced by the feminine values of 'attachment' and 'community'. The idea is not to replace a masculine discourse with a feminine discourse, but rather to transform the highly gendered contemporary discourse into one that privileges values of pluralism, inclusivity and equity for human beings. The attempt should be to transcend the conventional binary oppositions of war and peace, power and powerlessness, public and private, reason and emotion, independence and attachment, where the first set of values are typically associated with masculinity and the second with femininity.

Ann Tickner's suggestion to privilege the values of 'empathy' and 'community' in the political and economic behaviour of states contributes significantly to building a cooperative, inclusive and sustainable discourse on security. Encouraging a recognition of the need for 'interdependence as one part of human behaviour would enable states and civil society to view community building not as an aberration but as another dimension of international behaviour'.[39]

SUSTAINABLE SECURITY AND POSITIVE PEACE: MAKING THE CONNECTION

Sustainable security requires sustainable peace. In this context, it is instructive to draw on the work of peace and conflict studies' scholar Kenneth Boulding who says that stable peace refers to a 'situation in which the probability of war is so small that it does not really enter into the calculations of any of the states involved'.[40]

Boulding advocates a process that begins with 'conditional peace' and then transforms itself into 'stable peace'. 'Conditional peace is a relationship in which general deterrence plays a key role, although the possibility of stronger threats or even actual violence is maintained for crisis situations. . . . Stable peace is a relationship

[39] J. Ann Tickner, *Gender in International Relations: Feminist Perspectives on Achieving Global Security* (New York: Columbia University Press, 1992), p. 133.

[40] Kenneth Boulding, *Stable Peace* (Austin, Texas: University of Texas Press, 1978), p. 13.

between two states in which neither side considers employing force in any dispute between them. Deterrence and compellence backed by threats of military force are simply excluded as instruments of policy.'[41]

The notion of 'positive peace' is also useful in this context. Positive peace has come to be associated with conditions of social justice, gender equity, economic equality and ecological balance, with an emphasis on human relationships and how people act to fulfil their human needs. It requires not only that all types of violence (overt, structural and cultural) are minimal or non-existent, but also that the major potential causes ('root causes') of future conflict are removed. Crucial here are issues of democratic participation, human rights and gender equity.[42] Negative peace is defined as the absence of widespread, overt, violent conflict where other forms of violence—cultural (violence against women) and structural (poverty, institutionalized discrimination)—continue long after the guns have gone silent.

Drawing on the perspectives of women's groups from around the world, Donna Pankhurst in *Mainstreaming Gender: A Framework of Action*, highlights the following characteristics of a society experiencing positive peace:[43]

- An active, plural and egalitarian civil society
- Inclusive social and political institutions
- Inclusive democratic political processes
- Gender equality
- Transparent and accountable government

Such a definition of peace connotes that while political negotiations, arms control and confidence building measures do enhance the notion of security, sustainability hinges on more than this. It depends greatly on the perceptions, attitudes and motivation of

41 Alexander George, 'Foreword', in Arie Kacowicz, Yaacov Bar-Siman-Tov, Ole Elgstrom and Magnus Jerneck (eds), *Stable Peace among Nations* (Maryland: Rowman & Littlefield Publishers, 2000), p. 13.

42 Donna Pankhurst, *Mainstreaming Gender: A Framework for Action* (London: International Alert, 1999), p. 4.

43 Ibid.

human beings to transform a particular conflict. In the context of India and Pakistan, sustainability depends on the extent to which relationships and systems that perpetuate conflict and discontent are transformed. The transformation of 'enemy images' and perceptions of mistrust and hostility is a central element of sustainable security, because this alone can make a 'negotiated peace' sustainable. In fact, several scholars and practitioners now suggest that the success of a peace process should not be determined in terms of whether a settlement has been reached but rather in terms of how people in conflict have changed in ways that are constructive. A model of sustainable security would, therefore, be one which takes into cognisance the 'root causes' and negative perceptions and attempts to transform these through processes of conflict resolution and reconciliation.

In defining sustainable security through such a lens, the focus shifts to the *how* and the *who*. In other words, what processes, strategies and actors would need to come together in order to accomplish the goal of sustainable security?

THE ROLE OF CIVIL SOCIETY

Working towards a vision, as defined in the preceding pages, expands the role of civil society to include a range of short-term and long-term goals.[44] For security to be sustainable, its contours need to be shaped by plural approaches and diverse actors such as academicians, policy analysts, media persons, business leaders, NGOs,

[44] Ashutosh Varshney, in his book *Ethnic Conflict and Civic Life: Hindus and Muslims in India* (New Delhi: Oxford University Press, 2002), defines civil society as the 'space that exists between the state, on the one hand, and family life on the other, and that allows people to come together for a whole range of public activities, which are wholly or partially independent of the state'. It is seen as a 'non-state space', but not a 'non-political space' of collective life. Ernest Gellner in his book *Conditions of Liberty, Civil Society and its Rivals* (London: Penguin, 1996) defines civil society as the 'set of diverse non-governmental institutions which is strong enough to counterbalance the state and, while not preventing the state from fulfilling its role of keeper of peace and arbitrator between major interests, can nevertheless, prevent it dominating and atomizing the rest of society'.

women's groups, youth leaders, private citizen networks and conflict resolution practitioners.

Official accords fall short of transforming the 'roots' of a conflict because they cannot repair the psychological and emotional schisms created by years of mistrust and hostility. It is in this context that civil society actors play a significant role by facilitating face-to-face contact and regular communication so that ignorance and mistrust are transformed and durable partnerships (at the level of individuals, groups and nations) are built.

A formulation of security that is inclusive, plural, people-oriented and gender-sensitive is one that is sustainable and can truly make a people *feel* secure. This suggests that at the level of the individual, there is psychological and physical safety and civic freedom, which facilitate healthy human development; and at the level of the state, there is an environment where the threat, or option, of force and violence does not enter the mainstream discourse. In the context of Pakistan and India, the interface between sustainability and security foregrounds the following elements: strong civil society participation, the involvement of professional conflict resolution practitioners (people trained as facilitators, educators, conciliators, diplomats, etc.), regular communication between (and within) governments and civil society, a growing web of economic interdependence, and mutually compatible self-images that do not perpetuate enemy images.

This is where multi-track diplomacy comes in. In order to achieve sustainable security, there is a need to foreground the philosophy and work of diverse civil society tracks. The concept of multi-track diplomacy suggests that there needs to be active cooperation between governments and civil societies (and coordination of strategies, approaches and processes) toward the accomplishment of a shared vision, defined here as sustainable security.

CHAPTER TWO

Track Two Diplomacy: Possibilities and Challenges

Peace is a state of mind and a path of action. Peace is personal and political; it is spiritual and practical, local and global. It is a process and an outcome, and above all, a way of being.

LOUISE DIAMOND
President, The Peace Company, Vermont, USA

In the 1990s, 'protracted social conflicts' killed five million people worldwide,[1] and created close to 12 million refugees and 5.4 million internally displaced people.[2] According to the Carnegie Commission on Preventing Deadly Conflict, the cost to the international community of the seven major wars in the 1990s, not including Kosovo, was US $199 billion. This was in addition to the costs to the countries already at war (Sri Lanka for example).

The unimaginable violence and widespread devastation that have shaped the landscape of regions such as Kashmir, Sri Lanka and the Middle East have infused the consciousness of a whole generation with the question: Do governments have the resources and tools to transform conflicts between states and those within states? What has been the track record of official diplomacy in resolving protracted conflicts? With initiatives for conflict resolution, too often, coming a bit too late, and with old and new conflicts becoming more intense and violent, the need to search for sustainable approaches to security has become paramount. Over

[1] Patricia Brander et al., *COMPASS—A Manual on Human Rights Education with Young People* (Strasbourg: Council of Europe Publishing), May 2002.

[2] Adam Roberts, *Humanitarian Action in War* (London: International Institute for Strategic Studies, 1996), p. 12.

the last two decades, civil society groups have come to be recognised for their sustained efforts to build lasting peace and security in regions of protracted conflict.

THE EVOLUTION OF TRACK TWO

Peacebuilding initiatives undertaken by civil society outside the structure of government have been clubbed under the umbrella term track two diplomacy. Track two initiatives involve non-governmental, informal and unofficial citizen interaction between individuals/groups in conflict. Louise Diamond and John McDonald, co-founders of the Institute for Multi-Track Diplomacy in Washington DC, define track two diplomacy as the 'realm of professional, non-governmental action attempting to analyse, prevent, resolve and manage (intrastate and interstate) conflicts'.[3]

Historically, the notion of track one and track two diplomacy emerged from the realisation that formal, official, government-to-government interactions between instructed representatives of states were not necessarily the most effective methods of resolving conflicts and sustaining peace processes. Former American diplomat Joseph Montville coined the term track two diplomacy in 1981 to refer to the range of policy-oriented informal and non-governmental problem-solving efforts by experienced and informed private citizens.[4] Such actors include former diplomats, academics, NGO workers, educationists, media persons and even government officials participating in an unofficial capacity. Track two interventions are based on the assumption that unofficial discussions provide a flexibility not available in formal settings. This flexibility offers an opportunity to 'examine the root causes of, and the underlying human needs in, conflicts to explore mutually beneficial solutions

[3] Louise Diamond and John McDonald, *Multi-Track Diplomacy: A Systems Approach to Peace* (West Hartford, Connecticut: Kumarian Press, 1996), p. 4.

[4] The terms 'track one' and 'track two' have their origin in an article titled 'Foreign Policy According to Freud' by William Davidson and Joseph Montville, published in 1981 in *Foreign Affairs*. This article helped to raise awareness within the United States about the constructive roles that non-governmental actors could play in building peace and security. The article also initiated discussion on the relationship between official and unofficial activities.

and address issues not yet on the official agenda'.[5] An important feature of track two initiatives is that they are innovative, flexible in structure and, in most cases, confidential.

According to Sundeep Waslekar, founder, International Centre for Peace Initiatives, Mumbai, 'the goal of track two diplomacy is to prevent or resolve conflicts by influencing state policies, or build confidence between the polities they represent'.[6] Several track two initiatives also involve government officials in their private capacities, with the explicit intention of influencing public policy. What perhaps is most unique about such initiatives is that they can bridge the gap between official positions by serving as 'testing grounds' for new policy alternatives.[7]

While the objectives of track two efforts are usually defined as twofold—impacting policy and public discourse—the work of intermediaries in contexts such as the US-Soviet relationship, Northern Ireland, South Africa and the Middle East, has expanded the scope of such non-official efforts to also include the facilitation of a process that reduces or resolves conflict by improving communication and building relationship between a range of stakeholders. Several track two efforts, particularly those in the Middle East and between the two superpowers during the Cold War, provided a space for participants to be exposed to the thinking of the other side (and thereby generate a better understanding) about the issues sustaining the conflict. Such interaction also helped to decrease tension, fear and misunderstanding by humanising 'the other'.[8] In many instances, it also helped the vocabularies and concepts of analysts from the conflicting sides to converge.

[5] Louise Diamond and John McDonald, *Multi-Track Diplomacy: A Systems Approach to Peace* (West Hartford, Connecticut: Kumarian Press, 1996), p. 37.

[6] Sundeep Waslekar, 'Track Two Diplomacy in South Asia', *ACDIS Occasional Paper: Research of the Program in Arms Control, Disarmament and International Security* (Urbana-Champaign: University of Illinois, 1995).

[7] Navnita Chadha Behera, 'Forging New Solidarities: Non-official Dialogues', in Monique Mekenkamp, Paul van Tongeren and Hans van de Veen (eds), *Searching for Peace in Central and South Asia* (Boulder, Colorado: Lynne Rienner Publishers, 2003), p. 212.

[8] John McDonald, 'The Need for Multi-Track Diplomacy', Occasional Paper No. 9 (Washington DC: The Institute for Multi-Track Diplomacy, May 2000), p. 2.

Another significant role has emerged in the form of keeping the channels of communication open when official diplomatic relations plummet. In the past, governments have found track two diplomacy useful in getting an 'informal sounding' of the other side's intentions; and in some instances, it has also been helpful in brokering political agreements. In the Middle East peace process, for example, a Norwegian research institute was critical in laying the groundwork for the Oslo Agreements in 1993. In Tajikistan, a joint US-Russian task force of private citizens with experience in conflict resolution, sponsored by the Kettering Foundation, has brought together various Tajik factions to lay a foundation for formal negotiations.

THE KEY PLAYERS

The profile and expertise of track two actors are most crucial to the success of the initiative that they engage in. Academic and professional credibility as well as the personal bearing of the track two actors are important. The profile of people whose initial work shaped the field—Joseph Montville, Jimmy Carter, Harold Saunders, John McDonald to name a few—has informed the growing literature on track two. Intermediaries such as Carter and Saunders had been in government and had brokered peace agreements as track one officials. Once outside the formal government set-up, their close association with track one proved an asset in their work as track two intermediaries. However, today there are several track two practitioners who do not wield such influence. Their strength rests on their ability to impart conflict resolution skills and expertise to individuals and groups in conflict, thereby building and expanding the constituencies for sustainable peace and security.

Satish Kumar, a member of the Neemrana track two dialogue between India and Pakistan, notes: 'The success of the US-Soviet track two process provides an important insight on the profile of track two actors. The members need to be highly knowledgeable about various aspects and dynamics of the relationship. They need to be respected people with certain credibility and legitimacy. Because the purpose of track two is to influence the government and public opinion, its work can yield results only if the members have a high level of expertise and credibility with the government."[9]

Track two diplomacy, which has its origins in initiatives to de-escalate tensions between the former Soviet Union and the United States, has undergone a sea change since the end of the Cold War. There has been a significant shift in the profile of the participants and the intermediaries. In addition to academics, former diplomats and politicians, the field now includes trained and skilled conflict resolution 'scholar-practitioners'. The participant base has also expanded to include NGO workers, journalists, and educators. Many of them have backgrounds in psychology, religion and law. Others also have enormous experience in social movements and community action programmes and/or are associated with prestigious research institutions, universities and think tanks.

TRACK TWO DIPLOMACY BETWEEN PAKISTAN AND INDIA

The most prominent track two initiative between India and Pakistan is the Neemrana Dialogue. The first meeting of the group took place at the Neemrana Fort in Rajasthan, India, in October 1991 with support from the United States Information Service (USIS). In recent years, the initiative has received support from the Ford Foundation and German foundations. It comprises former diplomats, former military personnel, media persons, NGO workers, educators and academics from the two countries. They meet at least once a year in India and in Pakistan. The co-chairs of the meetings are M.K. Rasgotra and Niaz Naik.

In the initial years, the Neemrana group decided that there were certain core issues that should be discussed at every meeting. These include the Kashmir conflict, economic relations, the conventional arms race, nuclear proliferation and CBMs. Other issues that the group regularly discusses include cultural exchanges, easing of travel restrictions, media and industrial cooperation and trade. The meetings of the group begin with a discussion on the international

[9] An Interview was conducted with Satish Kumar (ed. *India's National Security Review*) in July 2004, New Delhi.

scenario and the domestic situation in the two countries so that members can better understand the constraints under which each country is operating. This is extremely important because it enables participants to understand the compulsions and dynamics of policy-making on the other side. The Indian and the Pakistani members brief their respective governments about the proceedings (particularly about any new ideas that might have been generated) after each meeting. The governments facilitate the dialogue by granting visas for the meetings.

The proceedings are informed by two ground-rules. First, the group does not engage with the media as a matter of policy. Second, members do not refer to any aspect of Indo-Pak relations in terms of its history. The assumption is that the members are aware of the interpretations of history by the other side and would achieve little by discussing different understandings of the tumultuous history of the two countries.[10]

In 1995, an interesting dimension was added to the work of Neemrana. The group decided to involve, in some of its meetings, specialists from the two sides; for instance, professionals with backgrounds in business, in trade and in science and technology, were invited to attend some of the dialogues and to meet with their counterparts from across the border. The attempt, in addition to facilitating communication between professionals working in similar fields, was to explore areas in which the two countries could cooperate. In so doing, the group was also broadening the dialogue by involving people who did not live in the metropolitan cities of the two countries. This aspect of the Neemrana initiative is very important because it has, as a result, emerged as a facilitator of substantive communication between professionals from the two countries, for partnerships in crucial areas such as trade and science and technology.

The discussions of the Neemrana dialogue have been well informed because of the high level of expertise and experience that its members bring to the group.[11] The dialogue has not been

[10] Satish Kumar provided this insight.

[11] Interview with Satish Kumar.

associated with a single position, nor has it been perceived as an advocate for a particular political point of view. The diversity of opinions that make up the group, serve as an important strength.[12] In fact, this has gained it credibility among policy-makers and hence enhanced its ability to influence policy.

The value of a group such as this also lies in the refined analysis and advice that it gives to the two governments, thereby emerging as a source for useful ideas and options and as a tool for communication between the governments. Another important source of credibility is the reputation of the participants and their personal acquaintance with policy-makers. Many participants have worked in government, or have had consistent access to policy-makers. This points to some important criteria that are needed for the success of a track two dialogue: access to officials, the trust these officials have in the track two group, and the longevity of the dialogue. Neemrana has cultivated its relationships with people in government, both in the choice of participants and in the contacts, written and oral, with officials in Islamabad and New Delhi that it has made. The low profile of Neemrana has, in particular, helped it to build trust among participants, and between participants and their governments.

Because track two dialogues such as Neemrana target those who are policy-makers or in the corridors of power in general, it is often argued that their reach is limited to certain segments of elites. However, it is precisely this feature of the dialogue that perhaps increases their influence among political decision-makers. The idea is that if people with great skill and high former position collectively generate ideas that might help break a deadlock, then their governments will pick up these ideas and use them to move forward.

The Balusa group is another significant track two initiative comprising leading opinion-makers from Pakistan, India and the USA. It is chaired by Shirin-Tahir Kheli who is the founding Director of the South Asia Programme of the Foreign Policy Institute, Johns Hopkins University, Washington DC. In June 2001,

[12] Conversations with Meenakshi Gopinath, a member of the Neemrana Dialogue, in July 2004.

this group made some significant recommendations to enhance relations between the two countries. It suggested a 'revival of working groups in all areas as agreed to in the 1998 Lahore Declaration with an institutional structure for some movement within a specified timeframe'.[13] Members of the group felt that without a timetable, there would be less incentive for the two bureaucracies to move forward. On the Kashmir conflict, the group states: 'Both sides could find an agreed formula whereby cross-border incursions could be reduced in conjunction with a reduction in the number of deployed Indian troops in Kashmir. This way, each side would achieve an important element for their respective domestic constituencies.'[14]

The Balusa group is primarily known for its efforts to build a partnership between India and Pakistan on trade in electricity. The group focuses on bridging the differences between India and Pakistan by exploring, in particular, the economic, environmental and energy interests shared by the two countries to discover areas of collaboration and confidence building. A major focus of the group has been a project that involves a natural gas pipeline through Pakistan and India—a project of large economic benefit to both countries.

The group has also been actively involved in research and writing as part of its efforts to impact political climate in favour of conflict resolution. One such initiative has been the publication of a book titled, *India and Pakistan: The Cost of Conflict, The Benefits of Peace*, by Major General Mahmud Ali Durrani, a member of the Balusa group. Bringing out the relationship between military expenditure and national development, the book makes a case in favour of the redistribution of resources from armed forces towards national development projects. Thus Balusa is playing a critical role in impacting public opinion on the peace process and addressing an important dimension of sustainable security. It has also prepared

[13] 'Make the Summit Lahore Plus', *The Hindu* (New Delhi: 9 June 2001).
[14] Ibid.

reports recommending the following 'safety nets', many of which have filtered into policy-making circles:[15]

- Military-to-military hotlines, which in the past have helped to defuse tensions.
- Efforts to ensure that the conditions, which existed in the months after the attack on the Indian Parliament in December 2001, do not re-emerge.
- Comprehensive analysis of why the Agra Summit collapsed and what can be done to ensure that future summits address the *issues* and *process* in a sustained manner.
- A meeting between the head of the Indian and Pakistani intelligence services (RAW and ISI) in a third country would be helpful in establishing a working relationship on cross-border issues.
- On nuclear issues, the group believes that there is a need for transparency in nuclear policy decision-making processes. Transparency, through pre-notification, is needed in the deployment of weapons.
- Greater education of the political leadership on what it means to own nuclear weapons is also advocated.

Another significant track two group is the India-Pakistan Soldiers' Initiative for Peace, comprising retired armed forces personnel from the two countries. Formed in 1999 by the Pakistan Peace Coalition, the initiative began with the visit of a group of retired Pakistani officers to India in January 2000 followed by a visit of retired Indian officers in March 2001. The delegations have communicated with the political and military leadership and diverse civil society groups in the two countries. What is unique about this initiative is that, in addition to impacting the overall relationship, it seeks to build a much-needed dialogue and understanding between the two militaries.

Another example has been the nuclear risk reduction talks led by the Delhi Policy Group and the Islamabad Policy Research

[15] 'Safety Nets with Pak: Not Working Satisfactorily', *The Hindu* (New Delhi: 13 April 2002).

Institute. The talks seek to develop 'a shared and agreed lexicon' on nuclear concepts such as 'minimum nuclear deterrence' and prepare the ground for bilateral negotiations between the two governments. The foreign offices on both sides have been regularly briefed on this initiative.[16]

What perhaps distinguishes the Neemrana initiative from other track two efforts is that it is the only example of 'sustained dialogue' between scholars and practitioners from the two countries. Regular meetings make it possible for participants to dialogue in a manner that enables them to move from 'talking at one another' to 'talking analytically together'. Commenting on the importance of 'sustained dialogue' in the US-Soviet context, Harold Saunders and Vitali Zhurkin note: 'Only repeated meetings could allow relationships to develop that provided the context for a deepening exchange of insights and analyses.'[17] 'The frequency (of the meetings) allowed participants to develop a cumulative agenda, to be carried forward from one meeting to the next. . . . Frequency allowed a common body of knowledge to develop so that differences of interpretation could be narrowed over time as those differences were discussed repeatedly in changing circumstances.'[18] Although this comment was made in the context of the track two process between the USA and the former Soviet Union, the insights it offers for the value of a process such as Neemrana are important. In fact, such an emphasis on sustained dialogue, points to the significant contributions that the non-governmental tracks can make to the peace process between Pakistan and India.

However, the Neemrana initiative has come in for considerable criticism for its inability to impact policy in any significant manner.

[16] Navnita Chadha Behera, 'Forging New Solidarities: Non-official Dialogues', in Monique Mekenkamp, Paul van Tongeren and Hans van de Veen (eds), *Searching for Peace in Central and South Asia* (Boulder, Colorado: Lynne Rienner Publishers, 2003), p. 213.

[17] Harold Saunders and Vitali Zhurkin, 'The Conduct of Sustained Dialogue: What Have We Learned? What Next?' in James Voorhees, *Dialogue Sustained: The Multilevel Peace Process and the Dartmouth Conference* (Washington DC: United States Institute of Peace Press and Charles Kettering Foundation, 2002), p. 374.

[18] Ibid., p. 376.

Comments Teresita Schaffer, Director for South Asia, Centre for Strategic International Studies, Washington DC: 'The big problem with India-Pakistan track two efforts is that while they have produced some interesting ideas and created very good channels of communication among the participants, in most cases, they haven't had much impact on government policy. They put some ideas in circulation and in the public domain, but it is difficult to verify how, if at all, they have influenced government policy. . . . Ultimately, the people who were reached by their work were not able to change government policy.'[19]

The critical evaluation also comes from a school of thought, which believes that track two efforts, which have a more specific objective, such as Balusa, are more likely to have greater impact than groups such as Neemrana, which address a broader range of issues. The argument is that track two efforts that have a specific objective will come up with more specific proposals, and these are more likely to lead to specific policy outcomes. For example, the Balusa group is working on the Iran-Pakistan-India gas pipeline project—a project that has the potential to substantially improve bilateral relations, if implemented. While Balusa has not yet impacted policy, its work on the pipeline project, which includes the publication of joint papers on the subject, has significantly influenced negotiations on the pipeline, which in turn could strengthen bilateral cooperation.[20] In fact, the joint statement issued by President Pervez Musharraf and Prime Minister Manmohan Singh following their meeting in New York in September 2004 made a mention of the proposed gas pipeline, which could emerge as the most powerful economic project on their agenda.

This school believes that larger-scale track two efforts such as Neemrana, which address subjects ranging from Kashmir to nuclear risk reduction, might not be as effective (if success is determined in terms of impact on policy) as other efforts that have focused on more specific issues. Teresita Schaffer notes: 'While one cannot yet cite impact on policy, the chances of success for smaller track two

[19] Interview with Teresita Schaffer, June 2004, Washington DC.

[20] These insights were provided by Teresita Schaffer.

efforts are much better.... Continuing to work with former officials on very general topics doesn't ultimately produce very much.'[21] Criticism also comes from quarters, which believe that while papers brought out by the Neemrana group have not emulated official positions, the official positions have not changed significantly because of these papers.

Members of the Neemrana initiative contest this and cite their work with respect to the peace process in Kashmir as having significantly impacted government thinking on the subject. In 1995, when tensions between the two countries were high, the group decided to meet with Kashmiris on both sides of the Line of Control and involve them in the dialogue. Following meetings in Islamabad and New Delhi (and trips to Srinagar to meet with leaders representing a range of political perspectives), the group wrote a joint policy paper outlining the options on Kashmir. It submitted this paper to the then Indian Prime Minister, Narasimha Rao, and advised him to announce a package for autonomy for the Kashmiris. In less than a fortnight, the Prime Minister announced in Parliament that short of *azadi*, the Indian government would be willing to give autonomy to the people of Kashmir. Then he added: 'The sky is the limit'.

Unfortunately, before this proposal could be discussed further and implemented, the Narasimha Rao government fell, and was succeeded by a series of weaker coalition governments. In 1996 Farooq Abdullah won the state election on the platform of the autonomy proposal. Following the passage of a resolution on autonomy in the Jammu & Kashmir assembly, he submitted the proposal to the BJP-led coalition government then in power at the centre. The government rejected the proposal.

What is, however, important from the perspective of the Neemrana dialogue, is that it had been able to influence the thinking of the Indian government on the question of autonomy in Kashmir, most visibly reflected in Narasimha Rao's statement to the Indian Parliament. Further, the group has been able to stay in touch with the aspirations of the people of Kashmir, and has been able to communicate these to track one.

[21] Interview with Teresita Schaffer.

A second important accomplishment of the Neemrana group is cited as the relaxation in travel restrictions between the two countries, which was carried out by Mr I.K. Gujral, the Prime Minister at the time. A third significant contribution has been the publication of joint papers on various issues such as Kashmir and military CBMs. These papers, which have generated creative and useful options on the subjects, were submitted to the two governments. Their usefulness, and more generally the work and advice of Neemrana, have been acknowledged on different occasions by the foreign ministers of the two countries.[22] In fact, through the publication of joint papers, both Neemrana and Balusa have produced some very useful and creative ideas. The recommendations of such papers are remarkable also because the authors—an Indian and a Pakistani—were able to build a consensus on issues such as the Kashmir conflict, cooperative aerial monitoring, the gas pipeline project, the costs of conflict and war, to name a few. The Cooperative Monitoring Centre at the Sandia National Laboratories in New Mexico, USA, is another significant initiative in this respect. Sponsored by the American government, since 1997, the Centre has brought together Indian and Pakistani analysts to study cooperative monitoring and joint arms control strategies, and write co-authored papers on a diverse range of security issues.

Another initiative by Neemrana was undertaken in May 2004 when a few Indian members of the group visited Pakistan and produced a joint paper on nuclear CBMs. This paper was submitted to the two governments before the talks on nuclear CBMs began in June 2004. Its impact on the proceedings of the 'composite dialogue' was the subject of discussion at the Neemrana group meeting in October 2004.

In addition to specific instances of impact on policy, Neemrana often provides a second line of communication for the two governments, and narrows the gap in perceptions about the conflict between track one officials and non-governmental actors. It does this by engaging in private consultations with the two governments,

[22] This insight was provided by Satish Kumar.

advising them on policy options, and informing them about the popular perception at the grassroots.

An important role that individual members of track two groups such as Neemrana and Balusa have played has been through articles and editorials in the print media in the two countries, which seek to garner support for the ideas generated in the meetings. By presenting creative solutions through articles in the media, they not only enhance their ability to influence policy, but also build constituencies that might support such ideas. It is important however to note that most of these articles do not attribute ideas to individuals or groups, but rather point to the general trend of the dialogue and the options that the two governments might want to consider. For instance, the articles do not advocate a 'Neemrana position'. They simply generate a menu of options on different subjects for policy-makers and civil society.

Another important aspect of the work of track two has been its focus on the economic dimension of the bilateral relationship as a means for pushing forward the larger political process. The most powerful economic measure is the Iran-Pakistan-India gas pipeline. The idea, which the Balusa group has spent a great deal of time developing, has the potential to transform economic relations between the two countries. The pipeline, of course, raises serious political risk issues and complex questions. For instance, how would the actual ownership of the pipeline be structured? Would it be owned by the three governments? Would it be privately owned? However, analysts believe that these are issues that can be managed. For instance, one suggestion is for business leaders and lawyers from the two countries to collectively work on three or four options on how to deal with the political risks involved with the pipeline. In addition, lawyers and policy-makers who have worked on similar partnerships in other regions of the world can be brought in to share their expertise. Frameworks can be discussed for dealing with the 'spoilers' once the project has been implemented.[23] What is also important is that track two has been able to get the two governments to engage with one another on this subject.

[23] This insight was provided by Teresita Schaffer.

Another track two idea was that the borders (between the two Kashmirs) should be made soft.[24] The idea was that such an initiative would boost trade on both sides of the LoC, in addition to pushing forward the peace process. It would enable Kashmiris to not just meet their relatives but to also initiate some form of economic interaction, even if it was a measure as small as the sale of apples across the LoC.

While the proposal for a Srinagar-Muzzafarabad peoples' bus—a gesture that can emerge as an important tool for reconciliation—was discussed several times during the Neemrana discussions and transmitted to the two governments, the original idea and the spadework for its implementation can perhaps be attributed to John McDonald, former American Ambassador and co-founder of the Institute for Multi-Track Diplomacy, Washington DC. John McDonald, who has been facilitating dialogue and conflict resolution workshops for Kashmiris (parliamentarians, women's groups, business leaders, etc. from both sides of the Line of Control in third countries, came up with the idea of a peoples' bus during a visit to Srinagar and Muzzafarabad in 2000. The idea captured the imagination of Kashmiris on both sides because it meant that they would be reunited with their families living across the LoC. McDonald began circulating the idea in 2000 through meetings with Pakistani and Indian embassy officials in Washington DC. He met with Maleeha Lodhi, the Pakistani Ambassador to the USA at the time. With positive feedback from senior officials in the two embassies, McDonald started communicating with the political leadership in New Delhi and Islamabad who gave an encouraging response. The media soon picked up the idea and several analytical pieces have since been published on the possibility of a 'peoples' bus' connecting Srinagar and Muzzafarabad.[25]

In 2004, the Indian and the Pakistani governments made a commitment to start the bus service. Currently, the process is stalled over the nature of documentation that the Kashmiris would need to have to cross the border. Yet the importance of the fact that

[24] Interview with Satish Kumar.

[25] Interview with John McDonald, June 2004, New Delhi.

India and Pakistan have reached an agreement to start the bus service should not be lost sight of. What is particularly significant about this example is that it highlights the ability of track two to generate creative and constructive ideas, which can enrich the official peace process. In fact, the Srinagar-Muzzafarabad bus service and the natural gas pipeline—two issues that can be attributed to track two—have the potential to substantially impact the peace process and lay the foundation for long-term peace and security.

Teresita Schaffer points to another significant dimension of the role of track two groups in India and Pakistan: 'When the two governments sit down to talk, they need to have a common storyline. They need to have a common menu from which they can choose what to talk about. This is where track two can play an important role by helping develop a common menu from which the two sides can choose what to talk about.'[26] In other words, track two can help the governments to *together* define the problem and the issues sustaining the conflict, as well as generate options for political, economic and military confidence building measures. This can lead to a more sustainable formulation of security between the two countries.

SUSTAINING DIALOGUE: LESSONS FROM THE AMERICAN-SOVIET TRACK TWO PROCESS

Although the term track two was used for the first time in 1981, the Dartmouth Conference in 1960, between private Soviet and American citizens, can be cited as the first track two initiative. Initiated by Norman Cousins, the editor of the *Saturday Review of Literature* (with the support of the US President Eisenhower), the Dartmouth Conference was the first non-governmental, citizen-to-citizen meeting between the USA and the former Soviet Union and was sustained for thirty years.

Dartmouth was one of a number of dialogues between Americans and Soviets during the Cold War. Others included the Pugwash movement, the Soviet-American Disarmament Study Group and the International Physicians for the Prevention of Nuclear War, to

[26] Interview with Teresita Schaffer.

name a few. Dartmouth was distinguished by the close proximity of its participants to the two governments.

The first Conference was held on the Dartmouth College campus in New Hampshire, USA in 1960. The pioneers of the Dartmouth track two process had enormous faith in the power of face-to-face meetings to change attitudes, transform conflictual relationships and solve problems. The Conference addressed a range of issues such as arms control, foreign policy, the nuclear relationship, public perceptions of the conflict, and improving the overall relationship by facilitating a better understanding of the other side.

The annual meetings comprised participants who, although outside the governmental structure, had unofficial ties with their respective governments. The objective of the meetings was to exchange information and ideas and to listen *actively* to the other side. These off-the-record Dartmouth Conferences enabled influential Soviets and Americans to set the stage for track one agreements on a range of subjects such as the banning of above-the-ground nuclear tests and the expansion of trade between the two countries.[27]

Outlasting the Cold War, the Dartmouth track two process metamorphosed from a group fostering dialogue between enemies to one that built partnerships between Russians and Americans to work towards peace in other regions of conflict. In the time since the end of the Cold War, Dartmouth has tried to reduce tensions in different conflict settings, most notable being the civil war in Tajikistan where the Inter-Tajik Dialogue, initiated by the Dartmouth group has emerged as a blueprint for 'sustained dialogue'. However, in the forty plus years since its conception, 'the essence of Dartmouth has remained unchanged—the belief in the importance of communication between peoples in conflict . . . the belief that a dialogue among people outside government can be useful.'[28] The work of Dartmouth (in the context of the Cold War

[27] Michael Shuman, Gale Warner and Lila Forest, 'Citizen Diplomacy', *In Context Quarterly* (Washington DC: Context Institute, Winter 1987), p. 35.

[28] James Voorhees, *Dialogue Sustained: The Multilevel Peace Process and the Dartmouth Conference* (Washington DC: United States Institute of Peace Press and Charles Kettering Foundation, 2002), p. 4.

and in regions of contemporary conflict such as Tajikistan) has reaffirmed the valuable role that citizen diplomats can play in narrowing the enormous information gap that usually exists between adversarial groups/states—a gap that fosters mutual fear and mistrust.

In his reflections on the various concepts and insights that have emerged out of the Dartmouth process, Harold Saunders points to an important contribution: the development of the professional and academic field of conflict resolution through a focus on dialogue rather than on traditional diplomacy or official negotiation. Commenting on the US-Soviet track two process, Saunders says: 'We sat down together as enemies, when there was virtually no serious dialogue occurring between our two governments. . . . It was one of the lowest points of the Cold War. . . . We dared to hope that our work might make some contribution toward improving the Soviet-US relationship. By focusing on the overall relationship itself, we shaped a non-traditional agenda. . . . We did not talk about our conflicts as disputes over technically defined issues. Rather, we have talked about them as deep-rooted human and political conflicts. More important, we talked about the resolution of these conflicts not simply in the diplomatic terms of negotiation, but also in human and political terms.'[29] Adds James Voorhees: 'The Dartmouth Conference influenced the course of the Cold War. . . . It was a channel that Washington and Moscow used to transmit information and clarify perspectives when official channels seemed insufficient. It influenced the thinking of participants who in their turn influenced both the course of the Cold War and relations between Russia and the United States since.'[30]

According to David Mathews, President, Charles Kettering Foundation and Richard Solomon, President, United States Institute

[29] J. Scott Lauby, *Dartmouth Conference Task Force on Regional Conflict Prevention and Resolution: Toward a New Russian-American Dialogue on Regional and Societal Conflict, May 24-29, 1992, Moscow, Russia,* Stenographic Record (Dayton, Ohio: Charles Kettering Foundation), pp. 15-17.

[30] James Voorhees, *Dialogue Sustained: The Multilevel Peace Process and the Dartmouth Conference* (Washington DC: United States Institute of Peace Press and Charles Kettering Foundation, 2002), p. 4.

of Peace, 'in theoretical and analytical terms, Dartmouth has yielded important insights into the dynamics of communication and influence in situations of conflict, inspiring such useful concepts as sustained dialogue and the multilevel peace process'.[31] Notes David Rockefeller, a participant at the Dartmouth Conference for close to thirty years: 'While I cannot claim that our meetings hold the key to understanding the end of the Cold War or explain why neither side resorted to the use of nuclear weapons, it is nevertheless my belief that Dartmouth made a profound difference in the relationship between the two superpowers.'[32]

According to James Voorhees, 'the access that Dartmouth afforded to policy-makers in both capitals, and the trust placed by policy-makers in the participants, made Dartmouth a potentially valuable conduit for information. This supplement to official channels of communication between two sides to a conflict is a significant contribution that a trusted unofficial dialogue can make.'[33]

WHY STUDY THE DARTMOUTH TRACK TWO PROCESS?

The Dartmouth track two process offers important insights about the limitations of official diplomacy and the role that multi-track

[31] David Mathews and Richard Solomon, 'Foreword', in James Voorhees, *Dialogue Sustained: The Multilevel Peace Process and the Dartmouth Conference* (Washington DC: United States Institute of Peace Press and Charles Kettering Foundation, 2002), p. xi.

[32] David Rockefeller, 'Preface', in James Voorhees, *Dialogue Sustained: The Multilevel Peace Process and the Dartmouth Conference* (Washington DC: United States Institute of Peace Press and Charles Kettering Foundation, 2002), p. xiv.

[33] James Voorhees, *Dialogue Sustained: The Multilevel Peace Process and the Dartmouth Conference* (Washington DC: United States Institute of Peace Press and Charles Kettering Foundation, 2002), p. 339.

Commenting on this aspect of the role that track two groups can play, former Soviet Prime Minister Evgeni Primakov said: 'The whole history of the Dartmouth meetings demonstrates the usefulness of such non-official groups. . . . Even the present formal contacts between the Foreign Ministry (of Russia) and the State Department (of the USA) do not exclude the necessity of non-official exchange of opinions, in particular between those people who have the capability to report their impressions and conclusions after such exchanges to the highest state officials.' Ibid., p. 361.

diplomacy can play in shaping and sustaining a peace process. Commenting on this, David Mathews and Richard Solomon write: 'Citizens outside government promoting sustained dialogue can become significant actors in helping to transform the most intractable relationships from enmity to mutual understanding. Indeed, their work can productively complement what governments do by addressing tasks that governments do not do well—such as changing conflictual relationships when conflict has deep human roots.'[34]

This is a useful insight for India and Pakistan because of the similarity in the nature of the conflicts: Both can be defined as protracted and intractable where a profound lack of contact and communication between the peoples of the two countries compounded the problem through the building of enemy images and deep-rooted prejudices about *the other*.

In this context, a comparative study of the Dartmouth process becomes important for the insights it can offer to the track two process, and more broadly, to civil society efforts for peace and security, between Pakistan and India. Listed here are some of the reasons:

- It is one of the first few successful forums for interaction between citizens outside government and holds important lessons for the potential of such dialogue to transform deep-rooted interstate conflicts.
- The Neemrana Dialogue, launched in 1991 with support from the United States Information Service, was inspired by the Dartmouth process.[35] In the early 1990s, Harold Saunders (one of the key players in the US-Soviet track one-track two process) was invited to interact with members of the

[34] David Mathews and Richard H. Solomon, 'Foreword', in James Voorhees, *Dialogue Sustained: The Multilevel Peace Process and the Dartmouth Conference* (Washington DC: United States Institute of Peace Press and Charles Kettering Foundation, 2002), p. viii.

[35] Sundeep Waslekar, 'Track Two Diplomacy in South Asia', *ACDIS Occasional Paper: Research of the Program in Arms Control, Disarmament and International Security* (Urbana-Champaign: University of Illinois, 1995), p. 6.

Neemrana dialogue so that the latter could draw on the experiences of the Dartmouth process (in terms of its methodology, its successes and its failures) to enrich its own efforts for peace and security between Pakistan and India.[36] At this meeting, Saunders shared with the Neemrana group insights from his book *The Other Walls* (which is informed by his experiences with the Arab-Israeli peace process and the US-Soviet relationship, as a track one official and later as a track two practitioner). The book brings forth the important role that misperceptions and the psychological barriers of suspicion, prejudice, rejection, and fear can play in sustaining a conflict, and calls for a new set of lenses through which to transform such situations. Its most significant recommendation is that track two efforts as well as broader civil society initiatives need to be foregrounded more substantially in the mainstream discourse on peace and security. In fact, the Dartmouth process is a prime example of how sustained track two dialogue can, in contexts of deep-rooted conflicts, 'erase stereotypes, enhance respect, change perceptions, deepen understanding and even generate empathy for others' positions or analyses'.[37]

- According to James Voorhees: 'The notion that discussions such as those that took place at the Dartmouth Conferences could influence the course of international relations runs counter to the traditional, realist paradigm of how states conduct their business with each other.'[38] It validates the perspective that dialogue among civil society actors can transform adversarial relationships between states.
- An important insight that Dartmouth offers is that 'citizens

[36] Satish Kumar provided this insight during an interview conducted in July 2004.

[37] Harold Saunders and Vitali Zhurkin, 'The Conduct of Sustained Dialogue: What Have We Learned? What Next?', in James Voorhees, *Dialogue Sustained: The Multilevel Peace Process and the Dartmouth Conference* (Washington DC: United States Institute of Peace Press and Charles Kettering Foundation, 2002), p. 371.

[38] James Voorhees, *Dialogue Sustained: The Multilevel Peace Process and the Dartmouth Conference* (Washington DC: United States Institute of Peace Press and Charles Kettering Foundation, 2002), p. 5.

outside government can talk productively even in the context of a hostile and intensely competitive relationship between their governments. They can enlarge the picture of the overall relationship between whole groups or countries.'[39] 'The deeper picture of the overall relationship between two bodies politic that can emerge in dialogue, enlarges and complements the picture formed in official diplomacy and negotiation.'[40]

THE METHODOLOGY OF SUSTAINED DIALOGUE: INSIGHTS FOR PAKISTAN AND INDIA

The Dartmouth Conference offers one of the most elaborate laboratories from which to draw insights for a range of contemporary conflicts, the relationship between India and Pakistan being one of them. Perhaps, one of the most significant insights from the Dartmouth process is the need for a well-thought-out methodology to guide the *process* of dialogue. This study argues that a similar focus on *process* needs to be put in place in the context of the conflict between India and Pakistan.

One of the most significant outcomes of the Dartmouth Conference was Harold Saunders' conceptualisation of a dialogue methodology, which came to be known as 'sustained dialogue'. Developed and refined over a period of more than 40 years, this methodology holds important insights for the 'composite dialogue' between Pakistan and India (particularly in terms of how a dialogue can be deepened and widened). The methodology has inspired dialogues in different regions of conflict, the most notable being the Inter-Tajik Dialogue.

Harold Saunders lays out the process of 'sustained dialogue' as unfolding through a series of stages (Figure 2.1). First is a period in which adversaries take the decision to engage one another in dialogue. In the second stage, defined as 'mapping and naming

[39] Harold Saunders and Vitali Zhurkin, 'The Conduct of Sustained Dialogue: What Have We Learned? What Next?', in James Voorhees, *Dialogue Sustained: The Multilevel Peace Process and the Dartmouth Conference* (Washington DC: United States Institute of Peace Press and Charles Kettering Foundation, 2002), p. 367.

[40] Ibid., p. 370.

Stage One Decision to Engage in Dialogue ***Stage Two*** Mapping and Naming Problems and Relationships ***Stage Three*** Probing Problems and Relationships to Choose a Direction ***Stage Four*** Scenario Building: Experiencing a Changing Relationship ***Stage Five*** Acting Together to Make Change Happen

Source: Harold H. Saunders, *A Public Peace Process: Sustained Dialogue to Transform Racial and Ethnic Conflicts* (New York: Palgrave, 2001), pp. 98-145.

FIGURE 2.1: MAPPING SUSTAINED DIALOGUE

problems and relationships', they pour out their grievances and anger, often directed at the other side. This is the stage at which participants 'dump' their grievances on the table and experience others' perceptions, feelings and identity while moderators (representing the conflicting parties) map the dynamics of the relationships in conflict. This stage ends when the group agrees that it should focus its energies on a particular aspect of the conflict. In other words, it realises that 'venting has reached a point of diminishing returns'.[41] The third stage—'probing problems and relationships to choose a direction'—addresses the problem in a manner that enables the group to reach a consensus on how it might be dealt with. Here the quality of the conversations changes as the 'parties begin talking more analytically about the problem'.[42]

In the fourth stage—'scenario building: experiencing a changing relationship'—participants start thinking 'together about steps that might enable adversaries to begin changing their relationship, ending

[41] Ibid., p. 381.
[42] Ibid.

violence and rebuilding their community'.[43] The focus is on designing an action plan that can serve as a 'vehicle for change'. The fifth stage—'acting together to make change happen'—brings participants to a place where they can share their vision and roadmap with diverse sections of civil society and track one. The action plan is usually put into the hands of those groups who have the capacity to carry it out. An important element for the sustenance of such a process is the capacity of the participants to listen to perspectives different from their own.[44]

Saunders notes that if the dialogue process is sustained, participants come to form relationships, which serve as the foundation for action. The dialogue can take place on any of several levels—the official level (where formal negotiations take place), the quasi-official level (track one-and-a-half), or at the level of the broader civil society (where sustained dialogue can be initiated among non-governmental actors). Add Saunders and Voorhees: 'As the dialogue evolves, experience tells us that it becomes possible to reach across the political spectrum and include a wider band of participants. . . . Participants must be able to speak from the heart as well as from the mind. Sustained dialogue cannot be another academic seminar. Participants must be willing to come to terms with their relationships. This requires a willingness to show emotions ranging from anger to compassion.'[45]

The idea behind the sustained dialogue methodology (adopted by the US-Soviet track two process) was not simply 'to change relationships in the dialogue room'; but to facilitate the process in

[43] Harold Saunders and James Voorhees, 'New Approaches from a Rich Tradition: The 1990s', in James Voorhees, *Dialogue Sustained: The Multilevel Peace Process and the Dartmouth Conference* (Washington DC: United States Institute of Peace Press and Charles Kettering Foundation, 2002), p. 294.

[44] For a comprehensive analysis of the 'sustained dialogue' methodology, see Harold Saunders, *A Public Peace Process* (New York: Palgrave, 2001).

[45] Harold Saunders and James Voorhees, 'New Approaches from a Rich Tradition', in James Voorhees, *Dialogue Sustained: The Multilevel Peace Process and the Dartmouth Conference* (Washington DC: United States Institute of Peace Press and Charles Kettering Foundation, 2002), p. 311.

such a way that these changed relationships transformed 'the relationship between groups in the larger body politic'.[46]

FOCUS ON PROCESS

The experience of the Dartmouth track two process and the evolution of the sustained dialogue methodology points to the need to look at *process* in addition to the *issues* that make a conflict intractable. In other words, the *how* of track two is as important as the *what* of such efforts. In the South Asian context, while there is a considerable amount of literature on the limitations of, and opportunities for, track two diplomacy, little has been written about the *how* of such processes.

Internationally, the growing discourse on track two diplomacy has led to the development of some very useful concepts and methodologies, such as interactive conflict resolution, analytical problem solving, multi-level peace process, and sustained dialogue. In order to arrive at a formulation of peace and security that is sustainable, this study argues that track two and broader civil society initiatives in India and Pakistan need to start looking at the process they use to achieve their goals. The process used to accomplish a certain goal (changing public opinion, for instance) can determine the extent to which this goal is achieved.

Over the last two decades, track two practitioners, in different regions of conflict, have used a range of innovative methodologies to build and sustain peace processes. John McDonald and James Notter identify three such broad methodologies: 'consultation', 'dialogue' and 'training'.[47] The primary task of track two consultants is to provide a context for individuals/groups in conflict to meet in their personal (unofficial) capacity, in an effort to collectively engage in the exploration of creative, non-violent solutions to

[46] Harold Saunders and Vitali Zhurkin, 'The Conduct of Sustained Dialogue: What Have We Learned? What Next?', in James Voorhees, *Dialogue Sustained: The Multilevel Peace Process and the Dartmouth Conference* (Washington DC: United States Institute of Peace Press and Charles Kettering Foundation, 2002), p. 382.

[47] John McDonald and James Notter, 'Track Two Diplomacy: Non-governmental Strategies for Peace', *US Foreign Policy Agenda* (Washington DC: USIA, December 1996).

intractable conflicts. The significance of this methodology lies in the profile of participants it brings together. Usually the participants represent track one or are closely associated with it. Hence there is enormous potential to impact policy formulation. The most commonly used form of a 'consultation' is the problem-solving workshop, which enables participants to 'explore options without having to make commitments' and helps them to move beyond 'entrenched positions' to identify the 'real needs'. The meetings are usually closed to the media. The context provided for participants to build relationships with *the other* is an important attribute of this strategy.

The 1993 Oslo Accords in the Middle East are a prime example of this form of track two initiative. Here, a series of problem-solving workshops and dialogues between Israeli and Palestinian academics (facilitated by the Norwegians) paved the way for the signing of the Oslo Accords. Another significant initiative in this regard is the problem-solving workshop facilitated by Herbert Kelman at the University of Harvard with Israelis and Palestinians. Although participants attend the workshop as private citizens, it is significant that many of them are members of the official Palestinian and Israeli negotiating teams.[48] The problem-solving approach has also been used by track two practitioners like John Burton to address conflicts, which revolve around issues of recognition and identity. Burton used this technique successfully in the 1980s in the conflict between Christians and Muslims in Lebanon. The workshops, spread over a few years, were held at the University of Maryland. Each year, they brought into their fold a larger number of Christians and Muslims from Lebanon. Through a thorough analysis of the root causes of the conflict, the group made significant breakthroughs and generated creative options for coexistence, which filtered into policy-making circles in Lebanon.

Another significant track two tool is the 'facilitated dialogue group'. Here, intermediaries (third party or representing the conflicting sides) facilitate a dialogue between groups/states in conflict with the objective of opening up a space for building understanding and trust. These dialogue processes are extremely

[48] Ibid.

powerful when the participants are in a position to influence the thinking of governments. They are often used as a precursor to negotiation. Through the focus on intergroup and interpersonal relationships, the 'facilitated dialogue' provides a context for conflictants to learn and inquire and to truly 'meet the other'. This tool has been particularly useful in conflicts, such as those in Bosnia and in the Middle East, where official channels of communication have been blocked for long periods of time.[49]

Conflict resolution professionals also use the strategy of 'training' to empower groups to resolve and transform their own conflicts. This tool can impact various sections of society ranging from grassroots workers, private citizens, business professionals and academics to political and military leaders. Here the focus is on equipping individuals/groups with specific skills, tools and expertise in negotiation, dialogue, facilitation, reconciliation and conflict analysis. Like most track two initiatives, training programmes are designed to maximise the impact of the training on the conflict resolution process, particularly at the level of track one. The Institute for Multi-Track Diplomacy (Washington DC) and the Danish Centre for Conflict Resolution (Copenhagen) have conducted such trainings for Tibetan and Israeli diplomats as well as for UN peacekeepers. In doing so, they are creating a human infrastructure of men and women who have the expertise to support the non-violent transformation of conflict and build a durable foundation for peace and security.

It is important to point out that the tools of 'training', 'facilitated dialogue' and 'consultation', are often used in conjunction with one another. For instance, many 'dialogue' initiatives include 'training' in communication skills. These tools have also been used to achieve different objectives. On the one hand, they have facilitated substantive dialogue among non-official actors in a context where governments cannot participate directly and have thereby prepared the ground for track one interventions. On the other hand, by engaging groups independent of track one, they have contributed to broadening the discourse on security and building peace constituencies.

[49] Ibid.

TRACK ONE-TRACK TWO RELATIONS

The greatest challenge to, and perhaps opportunity for, track two lies in its ability to impact the thinking and functioning of track one. The overarching goal of any track two initiative is to help track one engage in a sustained dialogue or negotiation and/ or facilitate policy shifts. While track two efforts can build an environment conducive for a peace process to be initiated by track one, they cannot compel the latter to reach an agreement. Eventually track one has to yield results, since any formal agreement has to be negotiated, signed and ratified by the state and implemented by it. The important role for track two lies in building a commitment among government leaders to negotiate, and in preparing the ground for negotiation.

The relationship between track one and track two should be seen as symbiotic. This is because track one diplomacy (which is often based on power dynamics between instructed representatives of states) leaves little room for flexibility and for building consensus. By providing a context for track one officials to engage in their informal capacity as private citizens, track two intermediaries can help to transform threat perceptions and build bridges of communication and thereby support the work of track one.

The example of the Dayton Peace Accords, which ended the war in the former Yugoslavia in 1995 is important when looking at what track one can do and what track one cannot do. The track one negotiations, led by US Ambassador Richard Holbrooke, brought into place a much-needed ceasefire and political agreement in the former Yugoslavia. It was absolutely critical in terms of stopping the ethnic cleansing, which included widespread killing, sexual assault and forced migration. However, the Dayton agreement did not address the historical grievances or resolve the underlying sources of the conflict in the Balkans, which erupted a few years later in Kosovo.[50]

While track one by itself is unable to transform a conflict and build peaceful and secure societies, a peace process cannot move

[50] Kevin Clements, 'Civil Society and Conflict Prevention', *Facing Ethnic Conflicts* (Bonn: Centre for Development Research, 14-16 December 2000), pp. 18-19.

forward without the active engagement of this track. This is most visibly reflected in the fact that civil society interaction depends greatly on the extent to which track one supports it (particularly by removing travel and visa restrictions). For instance, in January 2002, the Indian High Commission in Islamabad issued only 30 visas to Pakistani citizens. The Neemrana group was unable to meet in 2002 and 2003 because of the dip in official relations following the attack on the Indian Parliament in 2001 and the subsequent mobilization of troops along the LOC. While the group continued to communicate via email and its Pakistani and Indian members met separately, clearly, its functioning was affected. In fact, in such times of crises, track two should be more active because the need to interact and clarify positions, interests and threat perceptions is much greater.

MEASURING SUCCESS

Social change has several causes. These are not always measurable. This presents a complex question: How do we measure success? How do we measure the impact of track two? The following questions could serve as yardsticks for measuring success. Has track two impacted policy? To what extent have official positions changed because of track two? Has track two helped to generate conciliatory gestures? Has it got the political leaders, religious leaders, teachers,

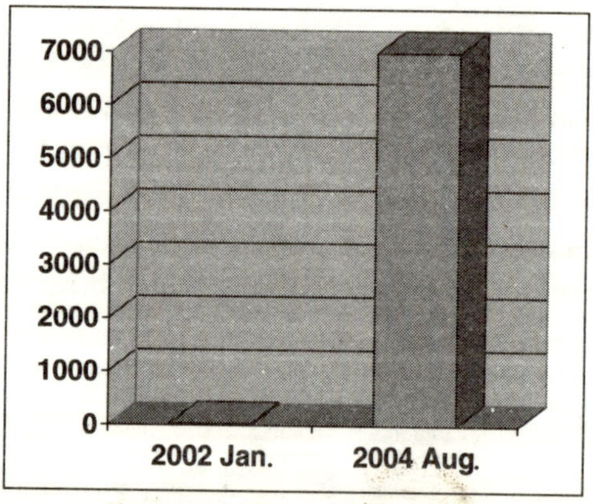

FIGURE 2.2: VISAS ISSUED BY THE INDIAN HIGH COMMISSION TO PAKISTANI CITIZENS

journalists, etc., thinking carefully about how they can build atmospheres conducive to non-violent problem-solving? Has it been able to reduce the levels and frequency of provocative rhetoric and acts of violence? Has track two been able to mobilise the opinions of the masses, particularly the younger generation (the 'future influentials')? Has it helped to de-escalate tension between states, such as India and Pakistan?

There is a growing realisation that track two can play an important role in 'knowledge creation', particularly by creating a body of knowledge regarding the cost-benefit analysis of bilateral and regional cooperation.[51] This can help policy-makers conceptualise more holistic and better-informed policies.

The concept of influence—central to the functioning of track two—is useful in this context. Influence is the 'ability to affect outcomes'.[52] Influence over policy can be gained through the transmission of information (to track one). According to James Voorhees, 'policy-makers need information about the intentions and capabilities of the actors with whom they deal; the policy they choose will depend on knowing whether the other actor is hostile or not, aggressive or passive. They get some of this information from intelligence sources, some from the media, some from diplomatic reporting, and a variety of other sources.'[53] Another important source of this information is track two.

The impact of track two on policy-makers can be assessed by 'examining either the direct influence on state policy or their indirect influence, that is, their ability to influence the climate of opinion in which policy is made'.[54] For instance, in the context of the Dartmouth track two process, members of the US Congress

[51] Navnita Chadha Behera, 'Forging New Solidarities: Non-official Dialogues', in Monique Mekenkamp, Paul van Tongeren and Hans van de Veen (eds), *Searching for Peace in Central and South Asia* (Boulder, Colorado: Lynne Rienner Publishers, 2003), p. 215.

[52] James Voorhees, *Dialogue Sustained: The Multilevel Peace Process and the Dartmouth Conference* (Washington DC: United States Institute of Peace Press and Charles Kettering Foundation, 2002), p. 11.

[53] Ibid.

[54] Ibid., p. 333.

took part in several of the conferences. Their participation created the potential for direct influence on individual legislators and indirect influence on Congress and the public as they communicated what they had learned at Dartmouth to their colleagues and constituents.[55] The Neemrana group transmits the results of meetings directly to policy-makers in both countries through written summaries, letters and meeting them formally/informally. According to Voorhees, 'indirect influence comes about when ideas or other pieces of information enter the general discourse on an issue'.[56] Track two groups such as Neemrana and Balusa have made a significant contribution in this respect through research and writing. However, the low profile nature of the groups does, to some extent, hinder their ability to impact the larger discourse.

The concept of indirect influence raises the question of evidence and verification. As Voorhees notes: 'How can one know whether one group or another has had influence on an issue? While it might be possible to discover how a policy-maker was exposed to certain ideas, what is more difficult is determining the source of the ideas. The objective of gaining influence, which links ideas and actions, takes us to the realm of what can be observed. . . . Efforts to determine the influence of an actor on policy, therefore, must often satisfy themselves with conclusions that are probabilistic.'[57]

However, Saunders and Zhurkin point out that 'the experience of the Dartmouth Conference suggests that it would be a serious mistake to judge such unofficial dialogues primarily in terms of their influence on governments.... That experience demonstrated a far more important perspective on such dialogues that is difficult for conventional evaluators and funders to grasp. In a historical perspective, it may be that the most valuable product was citizens with an alternative view of the world and of the relationship, and the abilities to articulate those views in ways that changed interactions between the two countries.'[58] The aim, in the first

[55] Ibid., p. 337.

[56] Ibid., p. 12.

[57] Ibid., pp. 12-14.

[58] Harold Saunders and Vitali Zhurkin, 'The Conduct of Sustained Dialogue: What Have We Learned? What Next?', in James Voorhees, *Dialogue Sustained: The*

instance, should therefore not necessarily be to impact government policy. Enabling citizens to conduct dialogues in ways that help them develop capacities and change perspectives can be an important goal in itself.[59]

The Neemrana initiative's conscious effort to work anonymously has been a double-edged sword. While this anonymity has enabled it to work successfully as a sustained back-channel force,[60] its decision not to engage with the mass media has reduced its ability to exert indirect influence—to affect the climate of public opinion. However, reflecting on his experience as a track one official and later as a track two practitioner, Harold Saunders notes: 'Anyone who has participated in the policy-making process will affirm that the "ideas in the air" do influence the way public officials approach a problem. . . . These "ideas in the air" often come from the private sector, especially when they reflect changes in viewpoint.'[61]

Decision-makers and bureaucrats share constraints that participants in an unofficial track two dialogue do not. 'The primary limitation is that decision-makers and bureaucrats (diplomats, soldiers, analysts) alike represent not themselves but their country and the particular government of which they are a part. By virtue of their position, officials must speak carefully and exercise caution before entering dialogues and relationships that take them outside the strict requirements of their positions. Informal conversation can be important, but it is used to explore the limits set by official positions.'[62] A sustained dialogue process such as Neemrana has the ability to step outside these limits, and explore, at a much deeper

---

Multilevel Peace Process and the Dartmouth Conference (Washington DC: United States Institute of Peace Press and Charles Kettering Foundation, 2002), p. 383.

[59] Ibid

[60] This insight was provided by Meenakshi Gopinath, a member of the Neemrana dialogue.

[61] Harold Saunders, 'When Citizens Talk', *Kettering Review* (Washington DC: Summer 1984), pp. 51-2.

[62] James Voorhees, *Dialogue Sustained: The Multilevel Peace Process and the Dartmouth Conference* (Washington DC: United States Institute of Peace Press and Charles Kettering Foundation, 2002), p. 14.

level, the perceptions and attitudes that lie behind the official positions of the two countries.

In the context of the US-Soviet track two dialogue, instances of direct influence include the achievement of a partial nuclear test ban treaty in 1963, the Soviet reappraisal of the American position on intermediate-range nuclear weapons in 1981, the reopening of US-Soviet talks in 1983 (and US-Soviet negotiations in the early 1980s), and the changes in the Soviet position on conflicts in the Middle East.[63] In fact, Evgeni Primakov, former Prime Minister of Russia, in later years, told Harold Saunders that these conversations had significant influence on the Soviet government, particularly on the official Soviet policy in the Middle East.[64] The Dartmouth dialogue was also able to leverage a considerable amount of indirect influence. Social and political concerns discussed at the meetings were not held tightly within the Dartmouth circle and did filter into public discourse.[65] Several participants, in their individual capacities shared these ideas and issues discussed at Dartmouth through newspapers, journals and books. Marshall Shulman, a participant in the Dartmouth track two dialogue notes: 'The transfer of ideas had a residual educational effect that you cannot always measure but which may be terribly important. There is a kind of diffusion of conceptions that goes on . . . there is an educational process.'[66] It is indeed difficult to measure the 'educational effect' of Dartmouth, but research conducted by James Voorhees and Harold Saunders does suggest that by affecting the climate of opinion within which policy-makers developed their ideas, Dartmouth did have a profound influence on the overall US-Soviet relationship.

In the context of South Asia however, Teresita Schaffer feels that 'the pattern in the India-Pakistan context, much more than in the Soviet-US experience, has been that track one officials do not lean terribly hard on their former colleagues in government, and at the

[63] Ibid., p. 345.
[64] Ibid., p. 347.
[65] Ibid., p. 348.
[66] Ibid., p. 351.

end of the day the government's policy does not change very much.'[67]

Track two diplomacy has been the subject of much criticism in recent years. The criticism stems from two concerns—the large size of the field and its elitist orientation. Because the field has not been institutionalised, it is difficult to define its contours. This has often led critics to define track two as a 'hat that has lost its shape'. The process looks elitist because of the profile of many of the intermediaries who were originally from track one. In the context of Pakistan and India, Navnita Chadha Behera notes: 'The tragedy of track two initiatives has been that by involving people too close to the establishment, by debating issues close to the governmental agendas and perspectives, and by trying to help the government through backdoor channels, they too (have) started reflecting the status quo governmental thinking.'[68]

There are several challenging questions that confront track two today. What is the role of a track two actor? Is it to build relationship or to achieve a tangible outcome? A major challenge facing the field today concerns the question of how an intermediary should deal with deeply embedded group psychological issues, such as those of insecurity, victimhood, forgiveness, etc. Navnita Chadha Behera points to an important flaw in the Indo-Pak track two process, which is the absence of 'institutional forums where track two professionals can report or brief government officials and policy-makers, along the lines of the track two processes connected with the Association of South East Asian Nations Regional Forum or the Council for Security Co-operation in Asia Pacific'.[69]

Criticism also comes from quarters that see track two as a dialogue between the 'converted'. There is a need for track two to engage with the hard-line groups and those who have a vested interest in perpetuating the conflict. Writes Sundeep Waslekar: 'If

[67] Interview with Teresita Schaffer.

[68] Navnita Chadha Behera, 'Forging New Solidarities: Non-official Dialogues', in Monique Mekenkamp, Paul van Tongeren and Hans van de Veen (eds), *Searching for Peace in Central and South Asia* (Boulder, Colorado: Lynne Rienner Publishers, 2003), p. 228.

[69] Ibid., p. 213.

track two diplomacy is to be meaningful, it must not only involve political decision-makers but also attract representatives of groups that are generally perceived to be opposed to conflict resolution.'[70] The Neemrana group has consistently attempted to do this, both in terms of the diverse political perspectives its members represent, and also in terms of its engagement with groups representing a cross-section of views in Kashmir.[71] 'One clear accomplishment, according to Waslekar, is that it (the Neemrana group) has opened new lines of communication between decision-makers in the two countries. . . . The Indian High Commission holds a reception for the Neemrana group, as does the Pakistani counterpart in New Delhi.'[72]

The ability to work during turbulent situations is an important yardstick for measuring success. This is particularly true in the context of India and Pakistan where periods of serene calm are few and far between. As Teresita Schaffer notes: 'If your process cannot handle turbulence, it is not ultimately going to create a breakthrough.'

Another source of criticism has been the failure of track two processes to emerge as the 'governmental instrument of choice or a major part of the diplomacy in the region'. 'Track two processes have almost never served as forums for surrogate or proxy negotiations occurring in concert with formal governmental negotiations, as they have, for example, in the Middle East peace process. Nor have they been used as a forum for discussing threat perceptions as part of a process of confidence building and mutual reassurance.'[73]

[70] Sundeep Waslekar, 'Track Two Diplomacy in South Asia', *ACDIS Occasional Paper: Research of the Program in Arms Control, Disarmament and International Security* (Urbana-Champaign: University of Illinois, October 1995), p. 9.

[71] This insight was provided by Satish Kumar and Meenakshi Gopinath (members of the Neemrana Dialogue) in interviews conducted in July 2004.

[72] Sundeep Waslekar, 'Track Two Diplomacy in South Asia', *ACDIS Occasional Paper: Research of the Program in Arms Control, Disarmament and International Security* (Urbana-Champaign: University of Illinois, October 1995), p. 8.

[73] Navnita Chadha Behera, Paul M. Evans and Gowher Rizvi, *Beyond Boundaries: A Report on the State of Non-Official Dialogues on Peace, Security and Co-operation in South Asia* (Ontario: University of Toronto/York University, 1997).

Despite these constraints, this study argues that in the context of India and Pakistan, track two diplomacy has made significant contributions to pushing forward the peace process and developing new ideas for sustainable security. Most importantly, it has a well-developed theoretical base and has motivated people to carry out its goals.

BUILDING LINKAGES: A NEW ROLE FOR TRACK TWO

Track two diplomacy has often been called the 'leading edge' of the multi-track diplomacy framework.[74] At a conceptual and practical level, intermediaries in this track can serve as a bridge between initiatives undertaken by governments and civil societies.

In order to more clearly articulate this important 'bridge-building' role that track two diplomacy can play, John Paul Lederach, drawing on his experiences in peacebuilding in regions such as Northern Ireland, Nicaragua, Tajikistan and the Middle East, conceptualized a model titled 'Actors and Approaches to Peacebuilding' (Figure 2.3).

This model (Figure 2.3) looks towards track two to provide the crucial link between the top-level leadership and the grassroots leadership in a context of protracted conflict. Lederach uses the term 'middle-range leaders' to refer to track two actors who he describes as 'persons who function in leadership positions within a setting of protracted conflict, but whose position is defined in ways not necessarily connected to, or controlled by, the authority structures of the formal government or major opposition movements'.[75] Such actors usually hold a position of respect and occupy formal positions in sectors such as education, academia, media or business. Their positioning is such that they are likely to be known by the 'top-level leadership' (track one) as well as have the respect and support of the constituency that the top-level leaders

[74] This term was originally used by Louise Diamond to demonstrate the significant role that track two peacemaking plays in the multi-track diplomacy system.

[75] John Paul Lederach, *Building Peace: Sustainable Reconciliation in Divided Societies*, (Washington DC: United States Institute of Peace Press, 1997), p. 41.

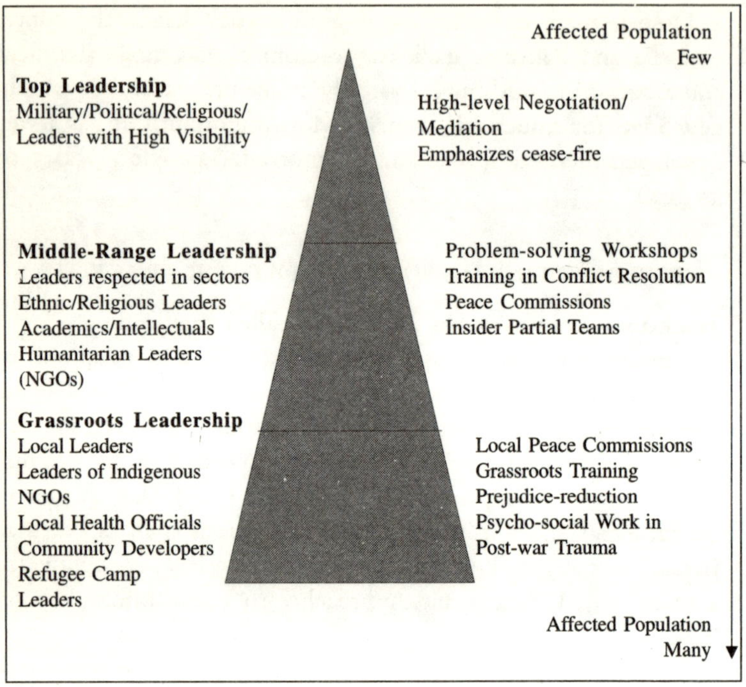

Source: John Paul Lederach, *Building Peace: Sustainable Reconciliation in Divided Societies* (Washington DC: United States Institute of Peace Press, 1997), p. 39.

FIGURE 2.3: ACTORS AND APPROACHES TO PEACEBUILDING
Reprinted with permission of the publisher.

claim to represent. They have contact with track one, but are not bound by the 'political calculations that govern every move made at that level'. Similarly, 'they know the context and experience of the people living at the grassroots, yet are not encumbered by the survival demands facing many at this level.'[76] Their unique location in a conflict setting enhances their ability to build sustainable peace and security.

Seen through this lens, in addition to impacting track one, track two actors can play an important role in building a civil society, which comprises a critical mass of informed, skilled and networked

[76] Ibid., p. 42.

non-governmental players who have the capacity to contribute to peace and security. Yet track two confronts an enormous challenge in conceptualising a mechanism that can inject the concerns and thinking of diverse civil society initiatives into interactions with people in track one. While track two actors, working in different conflict settings, recognise that efforts to build a synergy between the tasks of constructively engaging track one and building a vibrant civil society, present significant challenges, they are also aware of the powerful impact that such a role, if performed well, can have on the larger peace process.

While there is a consensus on the need for track two to play the role of a bridge-builder, at a practical level, few instances can be cited of it performing such a role. There is a general perception that track two groups in Pakistan and India function like 'elite clubs'. Further, there is very little interaction and cross-fertilisation of ideas between initiatives such as Neemrana and the Pakistan India Peoples' Forum for Peace and Democracy. If the contact does exist, it is sporadic and at the initiative of individual members. The US-Soviet Dartmouth experience offers important insights in this context. The Dartmouth Conference, till the late 1980s, had largely been a series of exchanges among elites. After 1990, Dartmouth began to evolve into a process involving broad sections of civil society. At the fortieth anniversary reunion of the Dartmouth Conference in September 2000, at the Institute of Europe in Moscow, the group discussed this new role it found itself playing. While Dartmouth continued its work with the political leadership, it also began to realise a need to 'cultivate the social and popular political levels' and engage with a cross-section of civil society.[77] Dartmouth thus moved beyond exchanges between elites around the intergovernmental agenda to embrace the idea of engaging a wide range of citizens outside government.[78]

[77] James Voorhees, *Dialogue Sustained: The Multilevel Peace Process and the Dartmouth Conference* (Washington DC: United States Institute of Peace Press and Charles Kettering Foundation, 2002), p. 331.

[78] Harold Saunders and James Voorhees, 'New Approaches from a Rich Tradition', in James Voorhees, *Dialogue Sustained: The Multilevel Peace Process and the Dartmouth Conference* (Washington DC: United States Institute of Peace Press and Charles Kettering Foundation, 2002), p. 278.

In so doing, it began to emerge as a bridge between track one and the civil society tracks, as well as a facilitator of dialogue and action between groups representing areas of common interest in the USA and Russia. In the context of India and Pakistan, it is crucial that track two build similar linkages, particularly with broader social movements (such as the women's movement). As Navnita Chadha Behera notes: 'The critical inputs for a new understanding of security are emerging from social movements, which although working in a local context, are sensitive to the wider picture. They raise fundamentally important issues concerning the possibilities of forging new solidarities, which transcend the boundaries of blocs and states and promote international cooperation irrespective of state policies.'[79]

[79] Navnita Chadha Behera, 'Forging New Solidarities: Non-official Dialogues', in Monique Mekenkamp, Paul van Tongeren and Hans van de Veen (eds), *Searching for Peace in Central and South Asia* (Boulder, Colorado: Lynne Rienner Publishers, 2003), p. 228.

CHAPTER THREE

Multi-Track Diplomacy: An Integrated Framework for Sustainable Security

Change more often seems to swell from the bottom up rather than to fall from the top down.

HAROLD SAUNDERS
Former Assistant Secretary for Near Eastern and
South Asian Affairs, State Department, United States of America

When the late Egyptian President Anwar al-Sadat made his historic trip to Jerusalem in 1977, he spoke of the need to bring down 'the other wall'. Here, he was not referring to a physical wall but rather to a wall that constituted a 'psychological barrier, a barrier of suspicion, a barrier of rejection, a barrier of fear, of deception' between Israelis and Arabs—a barrier, which he described as constituting '70 per cent of the problem'.[1]

This statement, although made in the context of the Arab-Israeli conflict, offers an important insight into the conflict between Pakistan and India. The similarity between the two conflicts lies in their *protracted, deep-rooted and intractable* nature. This, in part, can be attributed to emotions such as fear, suspicion, mistrust, hatred and misperceptions, which have emerged as potent sources of insecurity in both contexts—sources that track one negotiations or even track two diplomacy cannot adequately address and transform.

[1] Harold Saunders, *The Other Walls: The Arab-Israeli Peace Process in a Global Perspective* (Princeton, NJ: Princeton University Press, 1985). President Anwar al-Sadat made this statement before the Israeli Knesset in Jerusalem on 29 November 1977.

The conflict between India and Pakistan can be described as deep-rooted and intractable because, over the last half century, it has created antagonistic patterns of thinking that have become part of the social fabric in the two countries. These patterns have been passed on from one generation to the next, to the extent that large sections of the population in the two countries share a sense of alienation and mutual distrust toward *the other*. Over time and with an increasing number of casualties, both countries' populations have absorbed the conflict patterns at a deep, intimate level.

In a deep-rooted conflict such as this, official negotiations and 'resolution' of the primary issues (such as Kashmir, cross-border terrorism, Siachen, etc.) represent only part of the solution. To build sustainable security, it is necessary to have a peace agreement on paper *and* an atmosphere where the people of each country stop considering the other as 'the enemy', and eventually build a relationship based on mutual understanding, trust and respect for the differences that exist between their polities. This calls for a process, which moves beyond the *issues* to focus on the building of *relationships* (human and institutional) and the healing of wounds from past wrongs (perceived or real).

The central issue here is social change and transformation, which requires the establishment of new patterns of behaviour and thinking, not just at the level of government, but in different sections of society. While track two initiatives play a significant role in this context, such broad-based social transformation requires the involvement of a vibrant and inclusive civil society and the adoption of coordinated multi-disciplinary and multi-level approaches to peace and security. Kevin Clements, during a study on the ways in which conflicts in the 1990s have been resolved, concluded that none of the final political solutions have shown signs of sustainability. He argues that 'there can be no final track one solution to problems, nor any final track two or track-one-and-a-half solution' till such time as 'integrated and coordinated responses to conflicts' are devised.[2]

[2] Kevin Clements, 'Civil Society and Conflict Prevention', *Facing Ethnic Conflicts* (Bonn: Centre for Development Research, 14-16 December 2000), p. 1.

Writing in the months after the end of the Cold War, Harold Saunders, in his book, *The Other Walls*, pointed to a critical need for a new approach through which to understand international relations. Introducing the contours of such an approach, he noted that it is important to focus 'not just on the capabilities and policy-making of individual states acting on other states, but also on the overall relationships among bodies politic'. He was advocating a need to move beyond 'objectively defined' state interests and to focus on the relationships among broad sections of civil society (not just on relationships between the political leadership). This, he believed, would expand the capacity to generate and guide social transformation.[3]

It is in this context that multi-track diplomacy has emerged as a useful conceptual framework through which to explore how a variety of stakeholders, who employ different yet complementary strategies, can build sustainable peace and security. Beyond the track two practitioners and NGOs that help governments to broker political agreements, there exist a diverse group of non-governmental interactions that contribute to the notion of sustainable security. While track two diplomacy focuses on impacting government thinking and action, multi-track diplomacy processes broaden the audience and the issues (that are considered important for resolution and transformation). Because of their inclusive and participatory nature, they have the potential to sustain social change by improving communication, transforming prejudices, foregrounding new issues and perspectives, and providing a context for track one to address the root causes of conflict and solidify peace agreements.

Recognising that the designation of track two no longer captured the diversity, complexity and depth of civil society initiatives, Louise Diamond conceptualised the term multi-track diplomacy in an effort to take forward the ideas of conflict resolution embodied in Joseph Montville's definition of track two diplomacy, and to make visible the peacemaking potential of different sectors of society,

[3] Harold Saunders, *The Other Walls: The Arab-Israeli Peace Process in a Global Perspective* (Princeton, NJ: Princeton University Press, 1985), pp. 163–4.

particularly those whose work has rarely been associated with the goal of building peace and security. The notion of multi-track diplomacy is based on the premise that citizens from a variety of backgrounds have certain skills and expertise, which can be used effectively to transform conflict situations, and support and enable governments to arrive at sustainable formulations of security.

With John McDonald, Louise Diamond founded the Institute for Multi-Track Diplomacy in Washington, DC. Together, they began the process of framing the numerous peacebuilding initiatives as part of a system and *conscientising* the various players of the inter-relatedness of their peacemaking activities undertaken through different mediums. In this context, they designed a nine-track model to highlight the diversity of actors and approaches to peace and security in intrastate and interstate conflicts. Originally, clubbed under track two initiatives, today these actors and approaches represent seven tracks. These tracks seek to facilitate a process that reduces or resolves conflict between groups/nations by improving communication and building relationship; and that decreases tension, fear and misunderstanding by humanising *the other.*[4]

Given the complexity of contemporary conflicts—the India-Pakistan conflict being a classic example—multi-tack diplomacy provides a useful framework because it is based on the assumption that no *one* person, group or activity can deliver peace and security on its own. Sustainable peace and security require different actors, functions, activities and levels of intervention that are diverse and interrelated. What this means is that relationships need to be built between people who are not like-minded and who might not hold similar concerns or pursue similar activities. For example, multi-track processes seek to build linkages between actors as diverse as business entrepreneurs, trauma counsellors, educators, journalists, women's rights activists, lawyers, politicians and government diplomats. In so doing, they bring into their fold a diverse range of civil society actors, thereby broadening the constituency for peace. Such a process is absolutely crucial if security is to be sustainable.

[4] John McDonald, 'The Need for Multi-Track Diplomacy', *Occasional Paper Number 9* (Washington DC: The Institute for Multi-Track Diplomacy, May 2000), p. 2.

In addition to the diversity in actors, multi-track processes also facilitate the adoption of different yet complementary strategies and mediums such as fact-finding missions, conflict resolution training workshops, seminars (with an expected outcome), research and publications (to impact the broader political discourse), networking and relationship building initiatives, trust and confidence building workshops, problem-solving workshops and facilitated dialogues with track one and civil society actors.

THROUGH A SOUTH ASIAN LENS

In the South Asian region, primarily four tracks have emerged—track one, which involves official, government-to-government diplomacy; track two, which comprises former diplomats, scholars, educators and media persons who, because of their expertise and eminence, wield influence with track one (and are particularly helpful in generating creative ideas and options for governments); track three, which engages a broad cross-section of society and focuses on the building of constituencies for peace and on the 'rehumanisation of the other' through dialogues between ordinary people. Often representing an 'alternative power source', such initiatives are not only non-state, but they also frequently problematise the state. They see civil society as existing in constant opposition to the state.

In recent years, track one-and-a-half, which can be described as 'official back channel interaction' has emerged as an important level of engagement. The endeavours undertaken by N.N. Vohra, who is the interlocutor of the Indian government with various groups in Jammu and Kashmir, and the role that former Home Secretary of India, Mr K. Padmanabhaiah has played, as interlocutor in the Nagaland peace process, are examples of such diplomacy. Such individuals are in track one-and-a-half because, though they have a government brief, they do not necessarily serve government officials and have some freedom to take positions that are different from those that are officially stated. They have the freedom to meet anyone, to collect varied ideas, suggestions, and proposals, and to explore different options 'independent of the rigid status quo mindsets of the serving bureaucracy'.[5] Track-one-and-a-half plays a crucial role in enabling the political leadership, on different sides of a conflict, to arrive at a common definition of the problem. This involves identifying the sources of conflict, the structures on each side that benefit from perpetuating the conflict and then creating an environment conducive for sustained dialogue. Track one-and-a-half can also play an important role in helping governments to develop a commitment to negotiate; making an assessment on whether a particular solution at a given time would be acceptable to the political leadership; whether the political leadership would be able to *sell* this solution to its constituencies; whether the solution would be acceptable to the leadership on the other side; and whether that leadership would survive politically if it accepts the solution at a particular point in time. While the dialogue in this track remains confidential, what is important is that communication at this level should never be blocked or sporadic. The confidential nature of the dialogue enables the participants to meet informally and move beyond stated positions to explore options and opportunities that the conflicting states might be in a position to consider. In the absence of sustained track one communication, dialogue at the level of track one-and-a-half becomes even more crucial and useful for governments.

This conceptualisation of multi-track diplomacy does not adequately reflect the diversity, depth, complexity and potential of civil society initiatives to build sustainable peace and security. Further, it fails to bring into its fold the important role that sectors such as business, media, education and grant-making organisations (sectors that are rarely associated with the task of conflict resolution) can play in building sustainable security. The nine-track model serves as a more useful conceptual framework for an analysis of the diverse approaches and actors that are needed to build sustainable security between Pakistan and India. It assumes that interaction, coordination and collaboration between diverse groups can strengthen peace processes in ways that prevent the recurrence of

[5] Comments made by Satish Kumar at a Conflict Transformation Workshop organised by WISCOMP in New Delhi in June 2003.

conflict and the failure of peace agreements. Multi-track diplomacy argues for paying more attention to the *process* of interaction between nations, as well as developing a particular kind of *relationship* conducive for building sustainable peace and security.

THE MULTI-TRACK DIPLOMACY FRAMEWORK

Louise Diamond and John McDonald symbolically place all the tracks in a circle, each connected to the other with track nine (communication) tying the other eight tracks together (Figure 3.1). The model lifts out the complexity of, and diversity in, peacebuilding undertaken by civil society and points to the need for a multi-disciplinary approach to sustainable security.

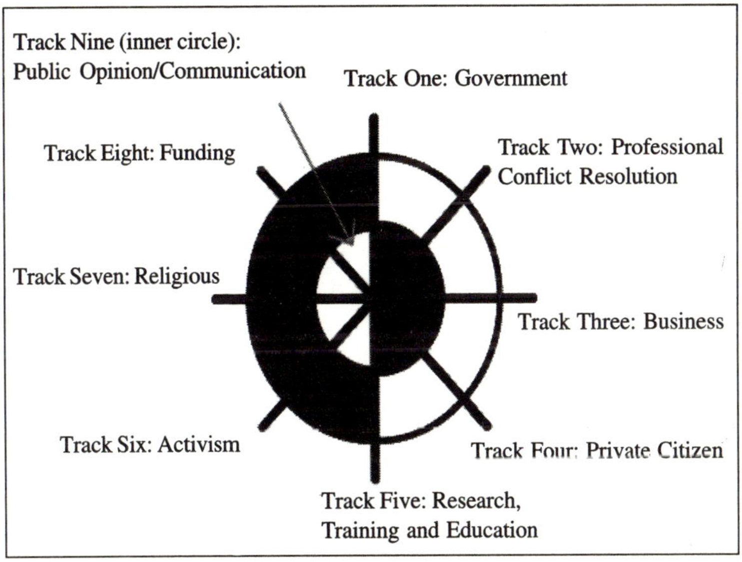

Source: Louise Diamond and John McDonald, *Multi-Track Diplomacy: A Systems Approach to Peace* (West Hartford, Connecticut: Kumarian Press, 1996), p. 15 (also available on the website of the Institute for Multi-Track Diplomacy www.imtd.org/about-theory-logo.htm).

FIGURE 3.1: MULTI-TRACK DIPLOMACY: THE SYSTEM AS A WHOLE

Reprinted with permission of the author.

According to this model (Figure 3.1), track three diplomacy—'peacemaking through commerce'—comprises the business community. The business community, through the medium of goods, services and partnerships, impacts peace and security by providing economic opportunities and by building pathways for goodwill and mutual respect. In recent years, this track has released significant financial resources to fund peacebuilding efforts in the other tracks. For instance, in 2001, a California-based information technology firm, jointly owned by a Pakistani and an Indian, sponsored a series of coexistence camps for young people from the two countries.

The PHD Chambers of Commerce and Industry India-Pakistan Desk, set up in 1982, has been playing a leading role in promoting business diplomacy between the two countries. It stays in close contact with the trade ministries and the high commissions in the two countries. It advises the India-Pakistan Joint Commission on Trade and arranges seminars and discussions on trade between the two countries.[6] In 2003, at the conclusion of a three-day visit by an Indian delegation to Karachi, Pakistan and India's Tea Associations signed a memorandum of understanding about increasing import of Indian tea to Pakistan from 3.5 million kg in 2002-3 to a minimum of 10 million kg in 2003-4. In July 2003, 150 Pakistani and Indian business representatives got together at the third and so far largest two-day meeting of the India-Pakistan Chamber of Commerce and Industry to discuss trade-related matters, in particular the low volume of bilateral trade. The meeting received widespread coverage in the media and was termed as 'the biggest-ever business delegation to India from Pakistan'. The group, with a focus on the promotion of bilateral trade and investment, held its first meeting in New Delhi in April 1999.

Currently, the official trade figure between India and Pakistan is about $260 million annually. There is tremendous scope for increasing trade between the two countries. For instance, Pakistan is the second largest consumer of tea and amongst the largest

[6] Navnita Chadha Behera, 'Forging New Solidarities: Non-official Dialogues', in Monique Mekenkamp, Paul van Tongeren and Hans van de Veen (eds), *Searching for Peace in Central and South Asia* (Boulder, Colorado: Lynne Rienner Publishers, 2003), p. 216.

importers of tea in the world. It imports most of its tea from Kenya (a country on another continent!), while it could import the same tea from India. This would not only benefit India, it would also significantly cut costs for Pakistan. There are several factors, which make the case for an increase in trade between the two countries very strong. First, the geographical proximity will cut costs substantially. Second, because of the similarity in language, tastes, fashion, etc., traders will be able to find markets easily. Third, trade theory tells us that if countries do business with their neighbours, not only would the job market expand, it would also increase their gross domestic product (GDP). If there were unrestricted trade between India and Pakistan, it would increase their GDP by 3 per cent each. Fourth, sustained economic co-operation would increase the flow of foreign direct investment (FDI) in both countries. Currently, South Asia does not attract as much FDI as South-East Asia, primarily because it is seen as a region prone to conflict. Fifth, and most importantly, if the Indian and Pakistani business communities were able to invest in each other's countries, their ability and motivation to pressurise the two governments to resolve the conflict would increase substantially.[7]

As Teresita Schaffer notes: 'The more economic business is done across the border, the stronger will be the constituencies for peace.'[8] Adds Beena Sarwar: 'It is when people realise that their economies can benefit from peaceful relations that they will put the necessary pressure on their governments to sustain the composite dialogue.'[9]

A growing number of analysts are beginning to look to the business community in the two countries as having the potential to push forward the peace process in ways that are mutually beneficial and sustainable. There is now a recognition that entrepreneurs and traders, by initiating economic partnerships, can build bridges across the divide. In fact, if Indian and Pakistani

[7] These insights were provided by Saira Basim, Lecturer, Quaid-e-Azam University, Islamabad, at a Conflict Transformation Workshop organised by WISCOMP in New Delhi in September 2004.

[8] Interview with Teresita Schaffer.

[9] An email interview was conducted with Beena Sarwar, a journalist and women's rights activist based in Karachi, Pakistan in June 2004.

business leaders are allowed, in the coming years, to invest substantially in each others' countries, they can help create an environment where the desire to annihilate or bleed *the other* is subsumed by a motivation to see *the other* prosper and grow. Such a sensibility contributes to the growing realisation that realism, which views such economic interdependence as an undermining of state sovereignty, fails to provide useful models for sustainable security between India and Pakistan.

It is not the assertion of this study that greater economic interaction can be a substitute for the political process. One would certainly need to see at least the beginnings of a political breakthrough before the two countries can even think about a big increase in business. Nevertheless, business leaders can play an important role in building a constituency, in the two countries, for normalisation of bilateral relations. In fact, several conflict resolution NGOs have started engaging with business leaders in the two countries with the purpose of *conscientising* them about the potential of their peacebuilding role as well as training them in conflict resolution approaches and skills. Equally important, government officials in both countries have acknowledged that they are using trade as an important track in the composite dialogue effort.

Social change begins with the self. Although this belief informs the work of several actors in the other tracks, it is most visibly reflected in track four, which Diamond and McDonald define as 'peacebuilding through personal involvement'. Track four encompasses a variety of peace and development activities initiated by private citizens. These include citizen exchange programmes, special interest groups and private voluntary organisations. The principle that guides those who work in this track is that the building of personal relationships with *the other* is a first step in finding a common humanity and in building sustainable peace and security. This track also sees the goal of sustainable development as an important component of any peacebuilding initiative. As Louise Diamond and John McDonald note, the major assumptions of those working in this track are: 'Each person can make a difference. . . . We can take personal responsibility for changing our world. . . . When we have personal relationships with others, we inevitably find our common humanity and are not likely to view them as enemies.'[10] In the Pakistan-India context, such private citizen involvement has been given a boost with the re-launch of the Delhi-Lahore bus service in July 2003. This was a significant initiative undertaken by track one to facilitate a much-needed face-to-face interaction between private citizens in the two countries. Such a step certainly enhances the opportunities for face-to-face interaction between Indians and Pakistanis, which can go a long way in transforming stereotypes and prejudices. Private citizen exchange programmes that have been initiated since the opening of road, rail and air links in July 2003, are making it possible for a growing number of Pakistanis and Indians to *meet the other.*

Track five is defined as the educational component of the multi-track model, comprising research, training and educational activities. It consists of the whole range of universities that offer education in conflict resolution and peacebuilding as well as think tanks and NGOs that include a variety of research, analysis and study programmes. This is the community from which much of the conflict resolution theory and practice comes today. In addition, academic exchanges, in and across other disciplines, can also be clubbed under track five diplomacy. What is key here is that such exchanges (in diverse disciplines such as sociology, anthropology, law, etc.) are carried out with the awareness that they have the potential to impact broader efforts for peace and security. This track produces and analyses information for the rest of the 'multi-track system' and has often been referred to as the 'brain' of the system. While track five diplomacy includes research, analysis and study programmes, this paper lists those educational programmes that also include human interaction and sustained dialogue.

Figure 3.2 does not represent an exhaustive listing of track five initiatives between India and Pakistan. In addition to the initiatives discussed here, there are several exchange programmes between schools, colleges and universities in the two countries. However, only those initiatives that are sustained on an annual basis have been highlighted here.

[10] Louise Diamond and John McDonald, *Multi-Track Diplomacy: A Systems Approach to Peace* (West Hartford, Connecticut: Kumarian Press, 1996), p. 60.

Organisation/Institution	Location	Area of Focus
• Regional Centre for Strategic Studies (RCSS)	Colombo, Sri Lanka	Security Studies
• Women in Security, Conflict Management & Peace (WISCOMP)	New Delhi, India	Conflict Transformation & Peacebuilding
• Seeds of Peace	Maine, USA	Coexistence
• Youth Initiative for Peace	United World College, Singapore	Dialogue & Conflict Resolution
• United States Educational Foundation (Fulbright Commission)	India and Pakistan	Conflict Resolution
• Lady Shri Ram College and Kinnaird College	New Delhi, India and Lahore, Pakistan	Conflict Resolution and Mass Communication

FIGURE 3.2: TRACK FIVE INITIATIVES BETWEEN INDIA AND PAKISTAN

An important track five initiative was started by the Delhi-based WISCOMP (Women in Security, Conflict Management and Peace), which holds an annual Workshop in Conflict Transformation and Peacebuilding for university students, young researchers, practitioners and journalists from Pakistan and India. The workshops facilitate the building of trust and respect through face-to-face interaction, in addition to imparting knowledge and skills in conflict transformation. WISCOMP also conducts and facilitates collaborative action research on issues relating to conflict transformation and conflict resolution in India and Pakistan.

The United States Educational Foundation (in India and in Pakistan) also plays a significant role in this track. Through its annual Fulbright Conflict Resolution Programme, USEF provides an opportunity for Indians and Pakistanis to pursue graduate studies in the field of Conflict Transformation at the Eastern Mennonite University in the United States. The uniqueness of this initiative lies in the fact that Indians and Pakistanis study the field of Conflict Transformation *together*, and are provided with an opportunity to *together* apply their learnings to the conflict. Their academic engagements and professional development are enriched with opportunities to engage with each other's worldviews in ways that enable them to find common ground and explore partnerships for peace in the region.

This points to an important role that universities and institutions of higher education can play in preparing the next generation to address the problems of violent conflicts in the region. Jane Schukoske, Executive Director, United States Educational Foundation in India, notes that these institutions have the 'opportunity to expand traditional course perspectives by teaching their communities about innovations to build and sustain peace processes'. Further, by bringing together individuals from hostile communities/nations, many of these institutions provide a much-needed context for informal interaction and face-to-face dialogue between students. 'This dimension of personal transformation and its relationship with social change, that several universities address, is an important contribution to macro processes of transformation and reconciliation.'[11]

Some of the other initiatives that use this long-term, 'generational approach' to peacebuilding include the Seeds of Peace coexistence camps for high-school students from the two countries (Maine, USA) and The Youth Initiative for Peace (United World College, Singapore), which brings together high school and college students and has a built-in conflict resolution component. The Youth

[11] The Brandeis University in Waltham, Massachusetts, USA deserves mention here. The University gives scholarships to Israeli and Palestinian students as part of its efforts to 'sow seeds of change' in the Middle East. 'Making use of the opportunity that a peaceful environment at Brandeis presents them with, the students organise weekly dialogue groups to focus on issues that divide them as well as those on which they can find common ground. The dialogue is facilitated on the assumption that their futures are intertwined and that, as the next generation of leadership in Israel and Palestine, they have a responsibility to search for solutions that are inclusive and sustainable.' Jane Schukoske and Manjrika Sewak, 'Track Five Diplomacy: Roles for Higher Educational Institutions in Conflict Transformation', in Mizanur Rahman (ed.), *Human Rights and Globalisation* (Dhaka: Empowerment through Law of the Common People (ELCOP), December 2003) .

Initiative for Peace facilitates dialogue and conflict resolution training to improve communication and build respect, trust and friendship between the next generation of leaders in the two countries. Institutions of higher education such as the University of Karachi (Karachi) and the Jamia Millia Islamia (New Delhi) also deserve mention. They have been among the first few universities in the two countries to introduce courses on peace and conflict studies for Indians and Pakistanis.

The Regional Centre for Strategic Studies, Colombo, which started a summer school on arms control and conflict resolution for young journalists, researchers government officials and scholars from the South Asian region more than a decade ago, has been the pioneer of this long-term approach to peace and security. Many of the workshops now include largely Pakistanis and Indians, thereby providing a valuable context to discuss important issues and build relationships and partnerships. The significance of such civil society initiatives cannot be underestimated. As Sundeep Waslekar points out: 'For the younger generation (in the two countries) who have not personally experienced the traumas of partition, it is much more interesting to discuss the future than events in the past. . . . Young people look at problems in terms of what it means for their future.'[12]

This sentiment is most visibly reflected in a question that Prerona Prasad, an Indian youth leader, put to President Pervez Musharraf on a visit to Islamabad in March 2000: 'Why does our generation have to carry the baggage of your past?' It echoes the growing desire among young Pakistanis and Indians to have a different kind of future—a future based on trust, cooperation and mutual respect.

The work of such education and research initiatives that focus on 'future influentials' is informed by a growing awareness of the need to work on humanisation processes and introduce the fields of conflict resolution and peacebuilding to a different generation of Pakistanis and Indians (in the age-group of 15 to 35 years). This

[12] Sundeep Waslekar, 'Track Two Diplomacy in South Asia', *ACDIS Occasional Paper: Research of the Program in Arms Control, Disarmament and International Security* (Urbana-Champaign: University of Illinois, October 1995), p. 8.

consciousness has begun to influence several organisations and individuals who are increasingly working with the third generation in the two countries—a generation that will be in positions of decision-making and leadership ten to twenty years from today. By investing in the 'future influentials', these initiatives are successfully ensuring that the baggage of fear, prejudice and suspicion, carried by the first and second generation, is not transferred onto succeeding generations of Indians and Pakistanis.

The significance of peacebuilding through track five diplomacy has gained widespread attention in recent years. This is because it can make two valuable contributions, which are a prerequisite for sustainable peace and security. First, such diplomacy focuses on the next generation of leadership in the two countries. Second, it provides an opportunity for the next generation to not only build relationships at a more substantive and intimate level, it also imparts education in the area of conflict resolution and peacebuilding to this generation. Without such education and interaction, it is highly unlikely that the next generation leadership will approach peace and security issues any differently from the way the previous two generations have dealt with them.

The peace activism field—track six—comprises activities associated with issues such as human rights, social and economic justice, disarmament, and the environment. The Pakistan India Peoples' Forum for Peace and Democracy (PIPFPD) has emerged as an important example of peace activism (Figure 3.3). Its initiatives reflect mass sentiment and have a percolation effect, which is so deep and visible that track one is compelled to act on the opinion of the people it claims to represent. The Forum, which seeks to transform consciousness as well as social structure, and transcend geographical borders as well as the borders of the mind, originated from a growing concern among large sections in the two countries to break down the wall of silence and distrust.

The process began with the first meeting of the Forum in Lahore, Pakistan, in September 1994. The Forum was started by Tapan Bose from India and Mubashir Hasan from Pakistan with four issues on its agenda: de-militarisation (and de-nuclearisation after 1998), intolerance, globalisation, rights of minorities in both

- De-militarisation (and de-nuclearisation after 1998)
- The Kashmir conflict
- Rights of minorities in both countries
- Globalisation
- Tolerance and respect for plurality
- Issues relating to travel restrictions such as stringent visa regimes and police reporting procedures
- Strengthening of cultural and student exchanges

FIGURE 3.3: ISSUES ADDRESSED BY THE PAKISTAN INDIA PEOPLES' FORUM FOR PEACE AND DEMOCRACY

countries, respect for plurality (particularly with respect to political beliefs and convictions), and the Kashmir conflict. In fact, the discourse that Kashmir should be seen not just as a territorial dispute, but also as an issue that concerns the lives and aspirations of the people living on both sides of the Line of Control stemmed from the PIPFPD conferences.[13] The PIPFPD also addresses issues relating to travel restrictions such as stringent visa regimes and police reporting procedures.

In addition to the annual conventions that the Forum holds, it has supported various cultural and student exchanges between the two countries. The Forum has played a particularly important role in expanding the constituencies for peace by involving ordinary citizens in the peace process, and has chapters in both Pakistan and India. It has, in a sense, put in place a process that cannot be turned back. Such has been its strength in empowering peoples' voices. Providing a space for the articulation of diverse political perspectives, the Forum has also served as a springboard for several Indo-Pak peace initiatives.

The PIPFPD is often written off as a gathering that does not have a significant impact on the peace process. This criticism comes from quarters that believe that the Forum has little or no impact on government policy and has not changed the dominant discourse in the two countries in any substantial manner. Even if success is measured not in terms of impact on policy but rather in terms of transforming the broader political climate, a great deal of scepticism

[13] Interview with Beena Sarwar.

has been expressed on the Forum's ability to move beyond 'bringing peaceniks together'. While such meetings between 'peaceniks' are valuable for mobilisation, strategy planning and action, some analysts believe that the Forum is not likely to win any new adherence this way.

However, only an initiative such as this can build peace constituencies in the two countries and put into practice the notion of a 'public peace process'. As Navnita Chadha Behera notes: 'The Forum spreads the dialogue process horizontally', involving a broad cross-section of people, particularly actors from the grassroots. This includes people from diverse professional backgrounds as well, such as lawyers, writers, activists, business leaders, trade unionists, army officers, etc. Adds Behera, 'the sheer territorial spread of the PIPFPD in terms of its local chapters in different parts of the two countries remains to be matched by any other dialogue.'[14]

In many ways, PIPFPD can be seen as a broad-based, transformative movement. By allowing members to hold different convictions on their perception of the Indo-Pak conflict, it has enabled them to reach a consensus, and address shared problems such as those of poverty, repression, women's rights, etc. What is most unique about the Forum is that it is a 'joint endeavour' between the citizens of the two countries. At a convention in Bangalore in April 2000, there were nearly 600 people of whom 250 came from different provinces in Pakistan. The significance of this Convention also lay in its timing. The Convention was taking place after the Kargil conflict at a time when bilateral relations at the official level had reached their lowest ebb. Yet people-to-people interaction grew.

In addition to the fact that it represents the largest people-to-people initiative between the two countries, the uniqueness of the PIPFPD also emerges from its ability and desire to build a web of relationships between different sections of civil and political society, thereby 'opening up the process (to audiences) beyond conference

[14] Navnita Chadha Behera, 'Forging New Solidarities: Non-official Dialogues', in Monique Mekenkamp, Paul van Tongeren and Hans van de Veen (eds), *Searching for Peace in Central and South Asia* (Boulder, Colorado: Lynne Rienner Publishers, 2003), p. 224.

halls and seminar rooms'.[15] In fact, the co-chairpersons of the PIPFPD, Admiral Laxminarayan Ramdas from India and Abdur Rehman from Pakistan received the 2004 Magsaysay Award for Peace and International Understanding in recognition of their work to build a transformative peace movement in the two countries.

Drawing on religion as a resource for peace, track seven comprises the various faith-based engagements that bring together individuals/ groups torn by violent conflict. The religious community provides the 'spiritual impulse and the ethical foundation that though present in the other tracks, is most publicly articulated here'.[16] This track brings a higher dimension of understanding and feeling to the issues of war and peace. Diamond and McDonald note that interfaith dialogue and joint projects are an important aspect of the work of this community. One of the most prominent examples of such diplomacy comes from Guatemala where Norwegian church organisations were instrumental in facilitating the dialogue between the parties to the conflict. Church groups have also played a significant role in sustaining the peace process in Nagaland, India. The July 2004 visit of Indian spiritual guru Shri Shri Ravi Shankar (The Art of Living Foundation) to Pakistan on a 'peace mission' has generated considerable discussion on the role that religious and spiritual leaders can play in transforming perceptions about *the other*, particularly those surrounding religious identities. The first Indian 'spiritual master' to visit Pakistan, he met with a diverse group of actors such as politicians, business leaders, religious leaders and social activists. The growing number of pilgrim visits between the two countries point to the important role that faith-based peace initiatives can play in building a constituencies for peace. In 2003-4, track one facilitated these initiatives by granting visas to more than 11,000 pilgrims to visit religious shrines in both countries.

Track eight consists of the funding community—those organisations and individual philanthropists who engage in peacebuilding

[15] Beena Sarwar, 'Women's Role in Building Peace between India and Pakistan' (Montreal: Centre for Research and Teaching on Women, McGill University, 30 July–1 August 2004), p. 7 www.mcgill.ca/mcrtw/peace/resources.

[16] Louise Diamond and John McDonald, *Multi-Track Diplomacy: A Systems Approach to Peace* (West Hartford, Connecticut: Kumarian Press, 1996), p. 102.

by providing financial resources for many of the activities undertaken by the other tracks. This community is critical to the success of civil society initiatives because by laying out guidelines for the activities it will fund, it defines the critical issues and sets the agenda for many of the other tracks. Without its support, the peacebuilding role of civil society would be greatly constrained. The Ford Foundation, The Carnegie Corporation, the United States Institute of Peace, the Ploughshares Fund and the W. Alton Jones Foundation are some examples of organisations that support peace and security initiatives globally.

Track nine—the pro-peace media (print, film, video, radio, poetry, the arts)—is seen as a mirror of society, articulating the voices of all the stakeholders in the conflict. According to the multi-track model, this track manages the relationship vertically between the public and the decision-makers and horizontally among the various civil society tracks. The media can play a crucial role by mobilising public opinion and moulding the perceptions of policy-makers. According to Siddharth Varadarajan, Deputy Editor, *The Hindu*, New Delhi, the coverage of India in the Pakistani press and vice versa has been one of the most neglected and important aspects of the whole problematic of India-Pakistan relations.[17] Varadarajan believes that the media can play an important role in building constituencies for peace by putting out into the public domain a vocabulary that empowers citizens to move beyond the 'us versus them syndrome'. The widespread, positive coverage that the various multi-track peace initiatives between Pakistan and India have received (since the re-initiation of the peace process in 2003), have helped to humanise the conflict and thereby transform it at a mass level. Film-makers from the two countries have also used their skills and expertise to generate public discussion on issues such as disarmament, threat perceptions, prejudices and identity. Two documentary films deserve special mention for their efforts to change the lenses that Indians and Pakistanis use to understand the conflict: *War and Peace* by Anand Patwardhan and *Crossing the Lines: Kashmir, Pakistan and India* by Pervez Hoodbhoy and Zia Mian

[17] Comments made by Siddharth Varadarajan at a Conflict Transformation Workshop organised by WISCOMP in New Delhi in June 2001.

It is, however, important to note here that the media is a double-edged sword. The creed 'good news is no news' has often meant that the media devotes relatively less time and space to covering initiatives for peace or issues that address the positive dimension of the Indo-Pak relationship. This is particularly true of the vernacular media in the two countries. Because of the power it holds to distort and control information that the other tracks need to carry out their work, the communications track can also emerge as a bottleneck. Hence, the term 'pro-peace media' has been used to define this track.

In recent years, the English language print and electronic media have played a significant role in broadening the constituencies for peace by connecting with a range of civil society groups in the two countries. The extensive print and electronic media coverage of diverse multi-track initiatives ranges from reportage on a group of Kolkata-based fashion designers who showcased their clothes' collections at fashion shows in Pakistan in July 2003, (and used this opportunity to build concrete relationships, personal and professional, between designers in the two countries) to Bollywood blockbusters such as *Veer Zaara*, *Main Hoon Naa* and *Dil Pardesi Ho Gaya* that promote the principles of mutual respect and friendship between masses in the two countries. Although such films are not made with the sole purpose to humanise *the other*, they certainly do help to change the lenses that an average Indian or Pakistani uses to understand the people of the other country. Such films have been commented upon extensively in the print media because they mark a significant departure from the not-so-long-ago released Pakistan-bashing Hindi films.

While several media companies in the two countries have taken bold initiatives to push forward the peace process, the most notable has been the Pakistan-based Jung group of newspapers, which has extended support to various Indo-Pak initiatives, and most recently, was a key actor in the setting up of the South Asia Free Media Association (SAFMA). Leading the discussion on the new role of the media as peacemaker, SAFMA was conceptualised and nurtured by Imtiaz Alam of *The News* in Pakistan and K.K. Katyal from *The Hindu* in India. SAFMA was created with the belief that if journalists do their job better, they can contribute to peace and security in the region. It runs a web portal (www.southasianmedia.net), publishes a quarterly South Asia journal, and holds conferences across the South Asian region for journalists and civil society groups. While at one level, it facilitates interaction among journalists, at another, it provides opportunities for capacity building and networking so that journalists can improve their analysis of conflicts. Recognising the important role that prejudices and mindsets in the two countries have played in sustaining intractability, SAFMA plans to initiate exchange programmes for young journalists from the two countries.

What makes this initiative stand out is the role it sees itself playing (in addition to addressing issues relating to the media). The role is that of a peacebuilder. In 2003, SAFMA facilitated a dialogue between the political society in the two countries by bringing together 100 Pakistani and Indian parliamentarians, many of whom have since been in regular contact. By 2005, SAFMA plans to bring together Indians and Pakistanis working on a range of issues such as trade and human rights. In October 2004, its long-held demand for 'free movement' of journalists between the two countries was met with the Indian government inviting SAFMA to lead a delegation of fifteen Pakistani journalists to Jammu & Kashmir.[18] This was followed by the Pakistan government supporting SAFMA's invitation to twenty journalists from Jammu & Kashmir to visit the Pakistani side of Kashmir in November 2004. The journalists visited Mirpur, Muzzafarabad and Gilgit. This SAFMA initiative has been hailed as 'historic' because, for the first time in the history of the two countries, journalists from Jammu & Kashmir have visited the Pakistani side of Kashmir, and Pakistani journalists have visited Indian Kashmir. Such visits enhance the ability of the media (at least some sections of it) to report and

[18] SAFMA had been lobbying with both governments to allow Indian and Pakistani journalists to visit Pakistan Administered Kashmir and Indian Administered Kashmir respectively. It had raised this issue with Yashwant Sinha at the SAARC Foreign Ministers' Meet in Islamabad in January 2004 and later with Mahmood Kasuri and Natwar Singh in September 2004 during the Foreign Ministerial talks in New Delhi.

analyse the conflict in a more holistic, transparent and less-jingoistic manner.

The idea of SAFMA developed out of a growing concern among Pakistani and Indian media-persons about the restrictions imposed on their ability to interact – namely stringent visa regimes and restrictions on publications being sold across the border. The founding members felt that in order to enhance communication and partnerships between journalists in the two countries, it was important for them to recognise that the media had a role to play in conflict resolution and peacebuilding. The significance of such an initiative that connects media and peacebuilding cannot be underestimated. B.G. Verghese, renowned journalist and member of the Neemrana initiative, notes: 'Over eighty per cent of the questions asked in parliament are based on what newspapers and journals write. Ninety per cent of what foreign offices think comes from what they read in the media. The diplomatic reports, the dispatches from the ambassadors come much later.'[19] Perhaps most significant has been the communication that SAFMA has facilitated between politicians and journalists in the two countries.

The impact of such mediums on the peace process cannot be underestimated. Whether it is an Indo-Pak music video on peace and harmony, which the Pakistani rock band *Junoon* released on the independence days of the two countries in 2004 (and to which Naseeruddin Shah and Shubha Mudgal had lent their voices), or a Bollywood film on the same theme, the potential of such mass media to transform 'enemy images' and 'threat perceptions' among ordinary Indians and Pakistanis is enormous. They have the ability to strengthen the movement for better bilateral ties by expanding the constituencies for peace in the two countries.

It is instructive to highlight that peacebuilding may not necessarily be the primary objective of some of these tracks. For instance, profit is the primary goal for the business community and for the Bollywood producer who makes a film on Indo-Pak peace. The print media sees its role as one of informing the public.

[19] B.G. Verghese quoted in Sevanti Ninan, 'The Media as Peacemaker', *The Hindu Magazine* (New Delhi, 4 July 2004), p. 3.

However, the significance of including them as tracks lies in the fact that there are streams within all of these fields that also recognise their role in building and sustaining peace and security.

THE MULTI-TRACK DIPLOMACY FRAMEWORK: A CRITIQUE

The usefulness of the Diamond-McDonald multi-track diplomacy framework (Figure 3.1) rests in its emphasis on building a web of relationships between diverse stakeholders to strengthen efforts for peace and security. The framework points to the vast potential that lies in employing an interdisciplinary approach and in *conscientising* different communities (such as business, media, education and funders) about their peacebuilding roles (and the need for them to coordinate their diverse functions and activities).

However, an analysis of the framework in the context of India and Pakistan points to a need for significant modifications, in terms of the selection of the tracks and their relationship with track one. While Diamond and McDonald envisage an important role for the faith-based community, a study of the India-Pakistan relationship sheds light on the divisive and vitriolic role that religious leaders, on both sides, have played. While there is no doubt that faith resonates strongly for a majority in the two countries, a cautious approach needs to be taken in using the religion track because, on several occasions, the generation of hate speech and attempts at demonising and dehumanising the other country have emanated from this track.

While the building of linkages between the governmental and non-governmental tracks is crucial, what is also required is a closer look at the intra-state multi-track relationship. For example, while partnerships between educational institutions in India and Pakistan are valuable, there is a need for these institutions to interact more closely with the other tracks (such as the professional conflict resolution community, the media and the government) at the intra-state level.

An important addition to the framework (Figure 3.4[a]) is political society—the arena between the state and civil society—, which

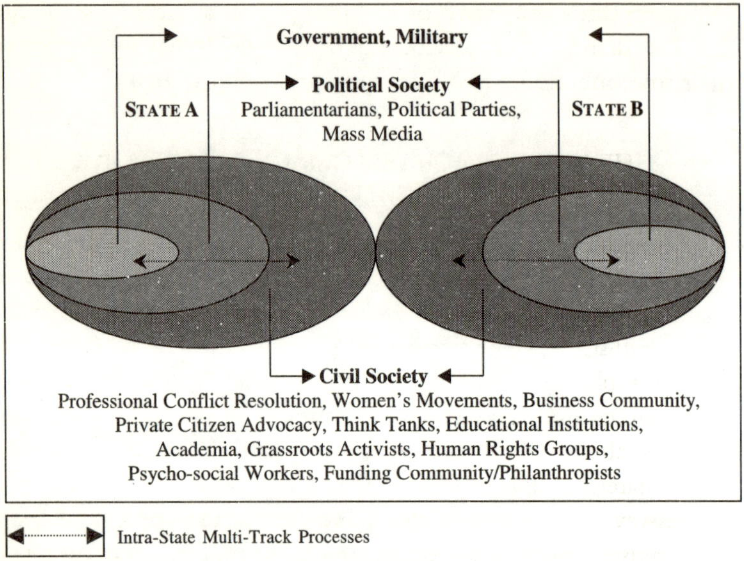

FIGURE 3.4(A)

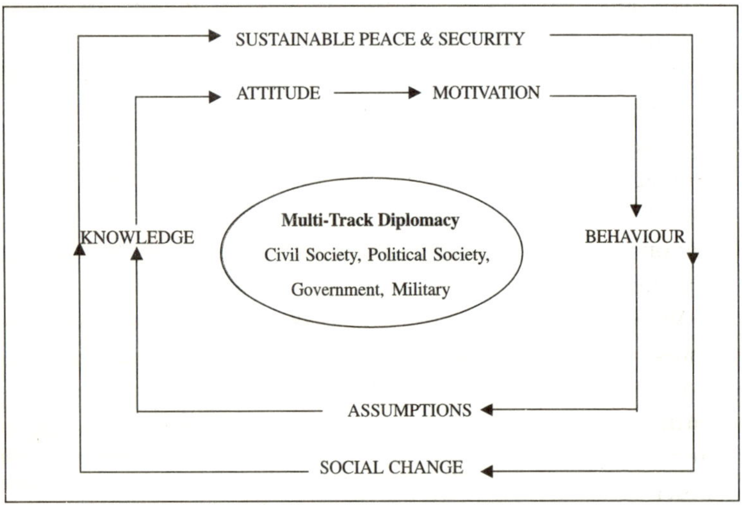

FIGURE 3.4(B)

FIGURE 3.4(AB): MULTI-TRACK DIPLOMACY: A FRAMEWORK FOR SUSTAINABLE PEACE AND SECURITY

includes political parties, parliamentarians and the mass media. The exchange visits between the chief ministers of the two Punjabs and between parliamentarians from the two countries are examples of the role that political society can play in strengthening multi-track efforts and impacting track one.

Another significant modification (as shown in Figure 3.4 [a]) relates to the positioning of the mass media track. While Diamond and McDonald see this track as lying at the heart of the multi-track framework, the specificities of the India-Pakistan relationship point to a need to look at the mass media as a *means* through which to strengthen multi-track processes and impact the thinking of governments, political leaders and opinion shapers. The overwhelming power of the mass media to transform public discourse and threat perceptions has already been discussed.

THE ROLE OF WOMEN'S GROUPS IN BUILDING SUSTAINABLE SECURITY

A significant exclusion of the Diamond-McDonald model (Figure 3.1) is the work of women's grassroots groups and feminist scholars in regions of protracted conflict. Women's groups, at the local and international levels, have played a significant role in developing sustainable approaches for conflict resolution. Particularly significant in this context has been the work of UNIFEM and the International Alert campaign on 'Women Building Peace: From the Village Council to the Negotiation Table'. The initiatives have not only brought more women into formal and informal peace processes, but have foregrounded the unique perspectives that women bring to formulations of peace and security.

Peacebuilding through women's movements can, therefore, be seen as an important track in the multi-track diplomacy framework. The women's movements in India and Pakistan have informed the larger peace movement by providing holistic perspectives on peace and security. Their focus on prejudice reduction and private and public violence, as well as their ability to transcend enemy-lines in the two countries, make them important actors in the peace process.

Cross-border collaboration and initiatives for peace and security between women's groups from Pakistan and India predate the work of the groups and networks described in the preceding pages. Communication and partnerships between women from the two countries can be traced back to the early 1980s. One of the first contacts between women's groups was in 1984 when Ferida Sher, then with the non-governmental Family Planning Association of Pakistan invited Indian peace activist Kamla Bhasin to Pakistan as a family planning trainer.[20] This was the beginning of a series of cross-border interactions among women from the two countries on a range of issues of common concern. A significant development in this respect was the 1988 Pakistani women's initiative (spearheaded by Shirkat Gah) to study the *Chipko* movement in India, which culminated in the first-ever joint Pakistan-India conference on environment in Lahore. This was the first event where Pakistani and Indian NGOs, government and media participated in an effort to initiate collaboration on environmental issues and concerns in the two countries.[21]

Perhaps, what has been unique about these interactions is that they have facilitated partnerships on a range of issues of common concern that women in both countries are confronted with – issues such as public and domestic violence against women, human rights, the environment, militarisation of the region and its impact on women's lives and livelihoods, etc. In addition to a recognition of the common issues that bring them together, there has also been a respect for the differences that arise from the existence of their historically formed identities.[22] Women's groups from the two countries have connected at various levels – the most striking being the similarity in the experience of violence in the family and in society. As Amrita Chhachhi, writing about the linkages built

[20] Beena Sarwar, 'Women's Role in Building Peace between India and Pakistan' (Montreal: Centre for Research and Teaching on Women, McGill University, 30 July–1 August 2004), p. 29 www.mcgill.ca/mcrtw/peace/resources.

[21] Ibid.

[22] Amrita Chhachhi, 'Of Knots and Weaves: Indian and Pakistani Women Connect Across Borders', *South Asia Citizens' Web* www.sacw.net/i aii/pag_a.html (August 1996).

between women from the two countries at the Fourth World Conference on Women in Beijing in 1995, notes: 'Indian and Pakistani women are subject to similar structures of patriarchal control within their families and communities. The greatest threat to women in both countries is from religious fundamentalist forces and the power they exercise over the state.'[23] These issues have built a strong bond between them, which in turn has paved the way for collaboration on initiatives to build peace and security in the region. Notes Beena Sarwar: 'Since the 1980s, Indian and Pakistani women have sustained cross-border friendships and associations, and retained the sense of solidarity developed initially during meetings and seminars. There is an unspoken resolve to abide by these friendships and continue the dialogue, regardless of political differences and opinions.'[24]

In fact, the collaboration between women's groups in Pakistan and India stands out for the ways in which they define security, and the multiple levels at which they connect. Their focus is not simply on overt public conflict, but also on private violence, which accompanies public violence. Foregrounding the interplay between different categories of violence, they make the connection between direct violence, militarisation, misogyny, poverty and under-development in the correct belief that this complex relationship impacts any formulation of sustainable security. Writes Rita Manchanda, a journalist and peace activist from India: 'Women's mobilisation against the arms race, military spending and nuclear testing is among the evidence of their long held view that military security is not synonymous with human security and is, in fact, detrimental to it.'[25] It is on issues such as these that women from the two countries have forged strong cross-border networks.

Feminist peace researcher Carolyn Stephenson points to the 'relationship between the violence of nuclear war and military force,

[23] Ibid.

[24] Beena Sarwar, 'Women's Role in Building Peace between India and Pakistan' (Montreal: Centre for Research and Teaching on Women, McGill University, 30 July–1 August 2004), pp. 9-10. www.mcgill.ca/mcrtw/peace/resources.

[25] Rita Manchanda, 'Redefining and Feminising Security', *Economic and Political Weekly*, Vol. 36, No. 22 (Mumbai, 2 June 2001), p. 1956.

the violence that occurs in families, and the violence of unjust economic and social structures defended by military forces.'[26] As Rita Manchanda notes, 'women are more likely to see a continuum of violence because they experience the connected forms of domestic and political violence that stretches from the home, to the street and to the battlefield.' In fact, empirical studies of the post-Yugoslav and Israeli-Palestinian conflict confirm the linkages between militarisation, misogyny and domestic violence.[27]

Collaborative research between women from Pakistan and India has led to the emergence of path-breaking literature, which has changed the way Indians and Pakistanis understand partition. Feminist researchers in the two countries have attempted to look at partition through a lens that places people rather than grand politics at the centre of the events of 1947. They have studied it from the perspective of the families that were divided, the people who had to cope with the trauma and rebuild their lives, and the impact of the collective experience of dislocation and trauma on the consciousness of whole communities. Most notable has been the work of Veena Das ('National Honour and Practical Kinship: Of Unwanted Women and Children' in her *Critical Events: An Anthropological Perspective on Contemporary India*), Urvashi Butalia (*The Other Side of Silence: Voices from the Partition of India*) and Kamla Bhasin and Ritu Menon (*Borders and Boundaries: Women in India's Partition*) on the ways in which partition affected the lives of people on both sides of the border, particularly women, whose voices have never been heard before. The experiences of these women compel us to use a different set of lenses through which to understand the turbulent history of relations between the two countries. Feminist scholars such as Veena Das and Urvashi Butalia address important questions: What was the impact of partition on women? How do ordinary individuals and the two states remember the mass rapes and abductions of women during partition? What

[26] Carolyn Stephenson, 'Gender and the United Nations', in Ingeborg Breines et al. (eds), *Towards a Women's Agenda for a Culture of Peace* (Paris: UNESCO Publishing, 1999).

[27] Rita Manchanda, 'Redefining and Feminising Security', *Economic and Political Weekly*, Vol. 36, No. 22 (Mumbai, 2 June 2001), p. 1959.

meaning do they make out of this? How did the states and civil societies respond to this kind of gender-specific violence?

The work of Ritu Menon and Kamla Bhasin, which began as a compilation of the oral history of women who lived through the partition of British India in 1947 (and which led to the publication of *Borders and Boundaries*), was also informed by research conducted by Nighat Said Khan in Pakistan on the experiences of women in the former West Punjab and Sindh. Such feminist historiographies of the partition of British India foreground the gendered narrative of displacement and dispossession, and in so doing, 'emphasise that a representative history can only be written if the experience and status of one half of humankind is an integral part of the story.'[28]

The Institute of Women's Studies, Lahore, founded by Nighat Said Khan, deserves mention here. It brings together women from the South Asian region to study courses on gender studies, development and peace studies. What is particularly significant is the opportunity that the institute provides for women from Pakistan and India to discuss issues relating to gender, conflict and peace in ways that build understanding and mutual respect. Of the belief that action cannot be divorced from theory, and that activism is an important and indispensable element for social transformation, the institute works with a diverse group of women's NGOs, peace committees, human rights initiatives, youth forums and cultural and literary forums in the two countries.

Women's cross-border initiatives have also informed the broader peace movement between the two countries. Women have been able to mobilise themselves to inject their perspectives into the larger peace movement, thereby contributing to a more holistic, durable and inclusive discourse on security. For instance, the Lahore Convention of the Pakistan India Peoples' Forum for Peace and Democracy in November 1995, informed by the perspectives of women's groups in the two countries, urged 'the governments and civil societies of Pakistan and India to undertake measures to counter the adverse effects of foreign and domestic policies of a militaristic

[28] Ritu Menon and Kamla Bhasin, *Borders and Boundaries: Women in India's Partition* (New Delhi: Kali for Women, 2000), p. 10.

nature, reflected in the growth of a culture of violence, hatred and guns, an aggressive and communalised nationalism, a distorted model of masculinity, and an increasing sense of insecurity for citizens of the two countries.' The resolution proceeded to add that a 'citizens' monitoring group would be set up to monitor hate producing and sexist images of war and military prowess in the media of the two countries.'[29]

The proposition that women need to be involved in a more substantial way in the peace process between India and Pakistan is not based on essentialist definitions of gender, nor is it limited to a preoccupation with numbers or what has been termed as 'add women and stir'. While the goal of getting a 'critical mass' of women involved in the peace process is vital, this can only be a starting point. The challenge lies in building a discourse on peace and security that privileges the perspectives of both men and women, and that holds as central the values of coexistence, pluralism and inclusivity. Women and men have different experiences of conflict, which inform their perspectives on conflict resolution. Hence, the participation of both is needed if durable peace and security are to be achieved.

TRANSCENDING BOUNDARIES: THE WOMEN'S BUS INITIATIVE

In March 2000, 40 Indian women, representing different faiths, generations, and diverse professional and political backgrounds, embarked on a twelve-hour bus journey. The journey took them from New Delhi in India to Lahore in Pakistan. In May 2000, women from different parts of Pakistan embarked on a similar journey to New Delhi.

Representing the most public cross-border collaboration between women from the two countries, this initiative was led by veteran Gandhian Nirmala Deshpande and brought into its fold women representing the media, academia, activism and business from the

[29] Amrita Chhachhi, 'Of Knots and Weaves: Indian and Pakistani Women Connect Across Borders', *South Asia Citizens' Web* www.sacw.net/i_aii/pag a.html (August 1996).

Pakistan India Peace Demonstration at Jinnah's Mazaar in Karachi,
14 August 2003. *Courtesy*: Naeem Sadiq.

two countries. The idea of a 'women's bus for peace' germinated in 1999 during the Kargil conflict—a time when war rhetoric and political jingoism had reached a deafening pitch, and stringent visa regimes had made contact between the people of the two countries extremely challenging.

The significance of this initiative lay in its timing. It happened at a time (March and May 2000) when hostility between the two countries was intense (following the Kargil conflict in Kashmir in the summer of 1999), and bilateral relations had reached an almost all-time low. In such an environment, women's groups in the two countries were creating a space for themselves and were also contributing to the creation of an atmosphere for the building (and rebuilding) of human relationships and for substantive dialogue on contentious issues including the Kashmir conflict. The initiative, which was organised by WIPSA (Women's Initiative for Peace in South Asia), brought into greater focus the need to open the channels of communication between the people (particularly the third generation) of Pakistan and India.

It is important to highlight that this 'bus for peace' initiative was in many ways a personal journey and commitment that translated into civil society action. In addition to the miles, the women who were part of this initiative had travelled a great distance in terms of their own perceptions of the conflict and options for its transformation.[30] As the follow-up initiatives gained momentum in the months following the Indian women's visit to Pakistan, one began to notice two very important contributions that women in India and Pakistan were making to the peace process between the two countries. First, by providing opportunities for face-to-face interaction and dialogue, they were facilitating a much-needed humanisation of perceived others. Second, they were substantively engaging in multi-track processes through their sustained meetings with various track one officials (including Pakistani President Pervez Musharraf and the then Indian Foreign Minister Jaswant Singh), NGO workers, media-persons, the business community and grassroots' leaders in the two countries. Following the 'bus for peace' initiative, women's groups from the two countries decided to address some important concerns such as the need to look into the biases and prejudices in school curricula (about *the other* country), the need for a relaxation in visas and for the free exchange of print media between the two countries.

A study of the peace process between Pakistan and India points to another significant role that women have played in peacebuilding: They have been able to negotiate and transcend 'fault-lines' and sustain cross-border dialogue, at times representing the only group of civil society doing so. Groups such as WISCOMP and WIPSA have been consistent in facilitating such dialogue even when track one communication has been caught in war rhetoric and political jingoism and civil society dialogue has been irregular and limited. Despite these contributions, the voices of women remain absent from the negotiation table, even though their perspectives might help to make a negotiated settlement durable and lasting. This raises the question: To what extent can any 'composite dialogue' be

[30] The author, who was also a member of this delegation, gained these insights through extensive conversations with the other members of the delegation from India.

successful if it does not include the voices of half the population of the two countries? As experiences from regions such as Somalia, Northern Ireland, South Africa and Nagaland in India demonstrate, women do have the ability to produce turnarounds in conflict negotiations by conceptualising agreements that are more inclusive, community-based and more likely to be successful in the long-run. Notes Rita Manchanda: 'Women's experience represents an alternative reading of history, the possibility of non-violent ways of negotiating conflict and agency in reconciliation and peace.'[31] This is particularly true in the context of Pakistan and India where women's groups (such as the Women's Action Forum, the Women's Initiative for Peace in South Asia, the Institute of Women's Studies, Women in Security, Conflict Management and Peace, Zubaan Books, Women Unlimited, Jagori, etc.) have been at the forefront of movements calling for sustained dialogue and reconciliation.

The most significant quality of the women's initiatives between the two countries has been their ability to meld together theory and activism in a manner that contributes to a holistic understanding of peace and security. Further, their ability to engage in multi-track processes (through interactions with government interlocutors and with a broad cross-section of civil society) has enabled them to transcend the boundaries of nationality, religion, ideology, gender and class in their work to build peace and security between the two countries.

[31] Rita Manchanda, 'Redefining and Feminising Security', *Economic and Political Weekly*, Vol. 36, No. 22 (Mumbai, 2 June 2001), p. 1958.

CHAPTER FOUR

Multi-Track Diplomacy: Sustaining Social Change

In the midst of today's upheaval, give us a vision for tomorrow.

MUHAMMAD IQBAL

This chapter addresses the challenge of moving beyond the establishment of peace and security to exploring mechanisms for *sustaining* social change. John Paul Lederach suggests that for sustainable change, it is important to 'create a proactive process that is capable of regenerating itself over time'.[1] Such a process, to begin with, should 'integrate the emotional and psychological with the substantive concerns of people in conflict, the underlying belief being that more than *realpolitik* and statist diplomacy are needed to build societies supportive of sustainable transformation'. Further, this process will be durable only if it includes a web of peacebuilding efforts, undertaken by diverse civil society actors operating in different time frames. For example, the more short term, often crisis-driven, efforts undertaken through back channel diplomacy and track one negotiations are crucial, but not sufficient to build long-term security (as defined in Chapter One). Not only should these short-term efforts be supported by a web of medium-range and long-term initiatives, their methodology and purpose need to be informed by the longer-term vision of sustainable security.

This points to a need for the participation of a broad cross-section of society, which has the ability to develop inclusive, coordinated and durable strategies for peace and security. In the

[1] John Paul Lederach, *Building Peace: Sustainable Reconciliation in Divided Societies* (Washington, DC: United States Institute of Peace Press, 1997), p. 75.

context of India and Pakistan, this is where multi-track diplomacy can play a significant role. By building a web of actors, roles and relationships, multi-track diplomacy recognises that the task of building security must, in addition to track one, include a diverse range of actors such as private citizen diplomats, religious leaders, media-persons, conflict resolution practitioners, NGOs, grassroots leaders, academia, the business community, women's groups, and those involved in psycho-social work. Multi-track diplomacy also brings into focus the need for, in addition to developing political track one-level agreements, adopting a transformatory approach to conflict where root causes, relationships (at the psychological, social, economic, political and military levels) and long-term visioning for social change can be adequately addressed. In other words, multi-track diplomacy integrates the different roles and functions of diverse civil society actors with the different levels and layers of peace-building and the timeframes (short-term, medium-range and long-term) for these. In doing so, it particularly encourages those peacebuilding efforts whose outcome may not be visible in the shortrun (for example, six months or two years), but which significantly impact the long-term vision for peace and security.

In order to highlight the diverse actors, roles, functions, activities and timeframes that are needed to build sustainable peace and security, John Paul Lederach presents 'an integrated framework for peacebuilding' (Figure 4.1) in which he links the foci and levels of intervention (by the governmental and non-governmental tracks) with the different timeframes in which they occur. In addition to providing a unique set of lenses through which to examine the factors that sustain the India-Pakistan conflict, this model brings forth the crucial need for a multi-track approach by highlighting the web of diverse actors, roles, initiatives and levels of intervention required to build sustainable peace and security between the two countries.

Lederach introduces this model as providing an 'infrastructure for sustaining the dynamic transformation of conflict and the construction of peace'. Such an infrastructure is based on the framework of multi-track diplomacy, which draws attention to the diverse actors, relationships, roles, activities and mechanisms that are needed

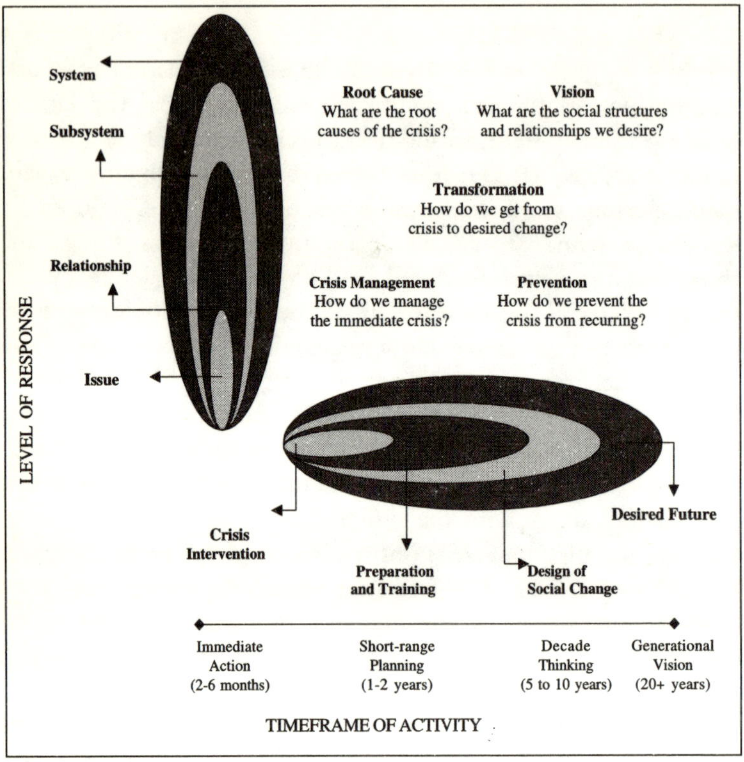

Source: John Paul Lederach, *Building Peace: Sustainable Reconciliation in Divided Societies* (Washington, DC: United States Institute of Peace Press, 1997), p. 80.

FIGURE 4.1: AN INTEGRATED FRAMEWORK FOR PEACEBUILDING
Reprinted with permission of the publisher.

to build sustainable peace and security. In Figure 4.1, the vertical axis reflects the diverse roles and functions for the governmental and non-governmental tracks, while the horizontal axis foregrounds the need to think of social change in terms of time-units of years and decades. As this figure indicates, the initiation and sustenance of social change requires diverse foci of interventions undertaken by different actors (government diplomats, educators, conflict resolution professionals, business leaders, trauma counsellors, women's groups, etc.) in different timeframes. For instance, an important function of track one is to resolve the central issues sustaining the India-Pakistan conflict (for example, Kashmir, cross-border terrorism, the nuclear relationship, Siachen et al.). Another important area is 'crisis intervention' where the immediate needs for ending recurring violence and human suffering or preventing the outbreak of war (which India and Pakistan came very close to in 2002), take precedence over other peace and security initiatives, but only in the short-run.

Sustainable peace and security, however, requires more than this. It calls for a systemic perspective where the 'root causes' and structures that sustain a conflict are transformed. This important function is often performed by track five, which includes academic and educational institutions and think tanks. Although not driven by the compulsions that immediate crises present, this track makes available to the government (and to the civil society tracks) important analyses, strategies and approaches for transforming the conflict-perpetuating structures in the long run.

Multi-track diplomacy also provides a space for engagement on 'conflict prevention'. For example, track two actors such as the Balusa group are making every effort to ensure that the standoff, which followed the December 2001 attack on the Indian Parliament does not recur. Taking a long-term approach to 'prevention', track five groups such as WISCOMP, RCSS and YIP (which provide education in conflict resolution and security studies, as well as a context for dialogue between Indians and Pakistanis) are building a much-needed capacity and motivation to prevent armed conflict between the two countries. The importance of such actors lies in their ability to think ahead in terms of time and develop analyses and capacity to prevent the outbreak of violence; or as in the case of India and Pakistan, to prevent the stalling or the derailment of the peace process.

Perhaps, the most significant dimension of the multi-track framework is its focus on the 'vision'. By foregrounding what Quaker peace activist Elise Boulding terms as 'imaging the future',[2]

[2] Elise Boulding, 'The Challenges of Imaging Peace in Wartime', *Futures* 23, No. 5 (1991), p. 528.

Lederach (in Figure 4.1) introduces a 'generational perspective' where our current approaches to peace and security are guided by the future we envision for coming generations. Such a concept compels us to think in terms of decades, and the social structures and relationships that we would want to see established twenty years from today.[3]

The work of tracks four, five, six and nine are particularly significant in this context. Track four (through its focus on building strong interpersonal human relationships with *the other* as a means for addressing contentious issues, transforming prejudices and promoting trust), track five (through conflict resolution training, educational events, peace research, and the production of textbooks on peace education), track six (through its emphasis on social justice and grassroots mobilisation as a means for transforming attitudes, policies and institutions), and track nine (which, in addition to the print and visual medium, includes those who Lederach refers to as the 'dream-keepers' – the poets, artists and musicians), contribute to the growing belief that 'the way things are is not the way things have to be'. Such multi-track actors, who Lederach defines as the 'visionary community', take the field of conflict resolution beyond the level of the intellectual relationship to a plane that engages with diverse mediums to transform deep-rooted prejudices, mindsets and relationships at the interpersonal, intercommunity, institutional and interstate levels. Perhaps the most profound initiative in this respect is the acclaimed *Ghoom Taana* musical short-film, which was released on the independence days of India and Pakistan in 2004. Conceptualised by Salman Ahmad, co-founder of the Pakistani rock-band *Junoon*, the short-film is the product of a cross-border collaboration between musicians, artists, film-makers, cinematographers and other media professionals. Featuring Pakistani rock musician Salman Ahmad, Indian classical singer Shubha Mudgal and Indian actors Naseeruddin Shah and Nandita Das, the film is a journey towards 'self-discovery and peace' where the 'universal face of humanity and culture, which transcends religion and politics' is

[3] John Paul Lederach, *Building Peace: Sustainable Reconciliation in Divided Societies* (Washington DC: United States Institute of Peace Press, 1997), p. 81.

Source: 'Salman of Junoon Visits His Ancestral House', *The Tribune*, Chandigarh, India, 23 February 2004.

Salman Ahmad (extreme right) in Patiala, India, during the shooting of the Ghoom Taana musical short-film. In this picture, he is with members of the family currently residing in the house of his mother's family. Courtesy: The Tribune

foregrounded. Reflecting on the role that the popular media (films, music videos, television and the arts) can play in building empathy between India and Pakistan, Salman Ahmad asserts: 'We need to stop intellectualising the relationship between India and Pakistan. People should see it with their heart and empathise with *the other*.... Peace is possible once we have deep empathy and compassion for *the other*.'[4] Adds Naseeruddin Shah: 'If this kind of melody cannot create harmony (between the two countries), then I really don't know what can.'[5]

Because of its ability to impact thinking patterns at a mass level, the *Ghoom Taana* project is a good example of peacebuilding through

[4] Salman Ahmad made this comment at a Conflict Transformation Workshop for Pakistanis and Indians organised by WISCOMP in New Delhi in September 2004.

[5] This comment was made by Naseeruddin Shah in a documentary film on the *Ghoom Taana* peace project.

track nine. However, it is also a powerful expression of the values that drive the work of track four: Social change begins with the self. Each person can take responsibility for transforming the antagonistic, conflict-perpetuating patterns at the macro level. *Ghoom Taana* is a manifestation of personal conviction transforming itself into a powerful political statement for peace between India and Pakistan. It draws inspiration from the true story of Ahmad's ancestors who migrated from Patiala to Lahore in 1947. The framework of multi-track diplomacy foregrounds the significance of such initiatives in transforming the conflict between India and Pakistan. Trust is a prerequisite for building sustainable peace and security, and a project such as *Ghoom Taana* opens up the floodgates for greater cross-border contact and collaboration, thereby facilitating the processes of trust-building, respect and friendship.

CHAPTER FIVE

Multi-Track Diplomacy: Looking Ahead

I am a world citizen who has to speak out for peace.

NIRMALA DESHPANDE
Veteran Gandhian and Peace Activist

There is a growing consensus that official-unofficial cooperation is an essential component of long-term peacebuilding processes. In part, this realisation comes from a recognition of the limitations of any single approach to build sustainable peace and security in contexts of protracted conflict, as well as the importance of both 'top-down' and 'bottom-up' approaches to conflict resolution.

It has come to be recognised that multi-track processes can create a fertile ground necessary for conflicting parties to reach a negotiated settlement. This is important because negotiated settlements will not hold unless a broad-based peace constituency supports them. A prime example of this is the importance placed on voter acceptance of the 1998 Good Friday Agreement in Northern Ireland.

Over the last decade, multi-track processes have helped to posit a worldview in which 'basic human needs and not just strategic interests have set the agenda in conflict settings; concerns relating to human security, not just the political side of world affairs, have received recognition; and international relations has begun to be seen as ongoing relationships between a diverse range of stakeholders, not crisis or situational relationships between states'.[1] A

[1] Interview with John McDonald, co-founder of the Institute for Multi-Track Diplomacy, in June 2004.

less visible, yet equally important, accomplishment has been the building of a shared vocabulary for coexistence among groups in conflict.

A significant contribution of multi-track processes has been the conceptualisation of the term 'positive peace'. While the work of many track two actors remains limited to providing analysis and advice to track one, multi-track actors have begun to redefine peace through their work. 'Negative peace', defined as the absence of war, suggests an emphasis on endeavours that reduce the potential of military conflict through arms control and disarmament. This notion of peace has its roots in how track one defines its purpose and role when attempting to resolve a conflict. 'Positive peace' refers to the conditions for social justice, economic equity and sustainable development through a focus on human relationships. It refers to 'an eradication of the culture of militarism and of structural violence. It is understood to entail a reordering of global priorities so as to promote economic development, participatory political processes and social justice.'[2] By so defining peace as such, multi-track initiatives have brought to the forefront issues that were hitherto considered insignificant by track one.

Multi-track diplomacy involves efforts that seek to change not only government policy, but also the way people think. This is extremely challenging because it means that the worldviews and basic attitudes of people need to undergo radical shifts for social change. In order to accomplish such a change, multi-track actors need to first, identify their audience; second, communicate with their audience effectively and relentlessly; third, coordinate their efforts with other civil society actors (and engage track one actors as well); and fourth, frame their ideas and strategies in ways that are well-organised and compellingly argued.

As we enter the 'citizens' century', multi-track processes confront significant dilemmas in terms of how they define their role and purpose. An important challenge relates to the question of funding. Since peacebuilding is a process, it is difficult to measure the

[2] Five College Program in Peace and World Security Studies, *Guide to Careers, Internships and Graduate Education in Peace Studies* (Amherst, Massachusetts: Peace and World Security Studies, 1990), p. 4.

outcome of a project or intervention. How can a potential funder be convinced of the need to invest in a project when there can be no tangible product to show, at least not for some years? How can relationship building between hostile communities be quantified and measured?

A second challenge relates to the interaction between track one and the civil society tracks. The interaction, which theoretically should be mutually reinforcing, is limited, sporadic and at times antagonistic. The challenge stems from the difficulty that all the civil society tracks experience in attempting to impact track one thinking and action. In fact, there is a tendency, in government circles, to describe civil society actors as 'naïve meddlers and amateurs' lacking skills and information to manage sensitive issues.[3] This tension, in fact, brings up questions about the very legitimacy and credibility of the civil society tracks. Louise Diamond and John McDonald note:'Important research produced by practitioners and theorists often goes unread by the official track. Trust developed and relationships built between conflicting groups through civil society initiatives, do not get transferred to those in a position to institutionalise these improved relationships. The religious community is easily written off by decision-makers as lightweight, yet it probably has the most extensive network on the ground in conflict areas. It has the best track record of successful behind-the-scenes intervention. The activist community is routinely de-legitimised by policy-makers, even though it has significant skills in grassroots organising and a profound awareness of the human aspects of policy issues. Citizens' diplomacy is often considered detrimental to the "real work" of diplomats.'[4]

Although the tracks exist independently, much of their work is ultimately about influencing and laying the groundwork for track one to initiate and sustain change processes for sustainable peace and security. Satish Kumar takes the view that while multi-track

[3] Navnita Chadha Behera, Paul M. Evans and Gowher Rizvi, *Beyond Boundaries: A Report on the State of Non-Official Dialogues on Peace, Security and Co-operation in South Asia* (Ontario: University of Toronto/York University, 1997), p. 32.

[4] Louise Diamond and John McDonald *Multi-Track Diplomacy: A Systems Approach to Peace* (West Hartford, Connecticut: Kumarian Press, 1996), p. 144.

efforts can build an environment conducive for a peace process to be initiated, eventually track one has to yield results, since any formal agreement has to be negotiated, signed and implemented by the state. The important role for the non-governmental tracks lies in not just building networks and constituencies that support the sustainable resolution of a conflict, but in also communicating to track one, their assessment of the situation and the various available options.

Mani Shankar Aiyar, a former Indian diplomat and currently a minister in the Congress-led coalition government in India, believes that although the official track often looks like a 'sound-proof tunnel with no light at the end', it is only this track, which can push forward a peace process. He believes that the role of the civil society tracks lies in signalling to track one that 'it should get going'. 'Stage setting'—preparing the ground for negotiation and creating an environment conducive for a peace process—and 'maintaining some kind of dialogue when track one is blocked' are really the key functions of the other tracks.[5]

An important source of divergence between track one and the civil society tracks is the lens used by the latter to redefine international relations. Where realists focus on the state and win-lose assumptions, multi-track actors focus on partnerships that transcend national boundaries. Writes James Voorhees: 'They are not concerned solely with governments but with how whole bodies politic—governments and other significant elements of society—interact. Where realists see a virtually complete absence of lasting cooperation, these actors examine other forces, such as ideas, personal relationships and domestic political structures.'[6] It is important to stress here that multi-track initiatives can be more effective if they engage with track one and build regular channels of communication with government interlocutors. They need to recognise that there

[5] Comments made by Mani Shankar Aiyar at a Conflict Transformation Workshop for university students from Pakistan and India, organised by WISCOMP in June 2001, New Delhi.

[6] James Voorhees, *Dialogue Sustained: The Multilevel Peace Process and the Dartmouth Conference* (Washington DC: United States Institute of Peace Press and Charles Kettering Foundation, 2002), p. 6.

are certain things that only governments can do. If they work without this consciousness, they will find significant roadblocks in their work. For instance, in order to change the relationship between India and Pakistan, there is a great deal of progress that governments need to make. Currently, the two countries have laws in place that make even basic communication difficult (stringent visa regimes, police reporting, ban on the sale of newspapers, to name a few). These are practices that only governments can change. Without such change, civil society interaction will be of a more adhoc and sporadic nature.

The relationship between track one, political society and the civil society tracks, which lies at the heart of the functioning of multi-track diplomacy, presents another complex challenge. Ideally, each track should take full advantage of the expertise, experience and resources of the other tracks. However, an analysis of the relationships between the different tracks suggests that although the tracks may define their tasks similarly, they often do not recognise that their work is related or that collaboration could enhance the impact of their efforts. The challenge, therefore, lies in exploring the interrelatedness of these tracks—how they support and strengthen one another and hence build sustainable peace and security. The civil society tracks, in particular, have the potential to operate more powerfully when they are coordinated and when see their roles as mutually reinforcing. For instance, in the India-Pakistan context, educators from the two countries (particularly those involved in teacher training) need to engage in substantive discussions among themselves and with other civil society tracks, in order to counter the vitriolic images of 'the enemy' that Indians and Pakistanis have internalised from a young age. More importantly, educators need to be *conscientised* about the valuable role that their profession can play in building peace and security for future generations of Pakistanis and Indians.

The lack of communication and coordination between the various tracks presents an enormous challenge. Writes Beena Sarwar: 'There is a lack of communication between peacebuilding initiatives, with no one organisation monitoring or recording the myriad activities taking place between the two countries. Groups visiting each others' countries often don't know that their peers have undertaken similar journeys, especially since many initiatives go largely unreported.'[7]

Despite these challenges, there is a growing recognition of the significant role that the non-governmental tracks and multi-track diplomacy can play in building sustainable security between India and Pakistan. The points that follow draw attention to some of the reasons why multiple civil society tracks are needed:

1. The conflict between India and Pakistan can be transformed only if the peace process is multi-layered, multi-disciplinary and includes diverse actors and approaches to peacebuilding. In this context, multi-track diplomacy has emerged as a useful framework through which to explore how a variety of stakeholders, who employ complementary strategies, can build sustainable security. Sustainable security requires not just a peace agreement, but also the sustenance of an atmosphere where the citizens of both countries stop considering the other as the enemy, and eventually build a relationship based on mutual understanding, trust and respect for the differences that exist between their polities. Such broad-based social transformation requires the involvement of a diverse group of multi-track actors who will be in a position to elicit the participation of stakeholders from a cross-section of the polity in the two countries.
2. Multi-track diplomacy broadens the audience as well as the issues that are considered important for transformation. There is, in fact, a growing consensus that official-unofficial co-operation and multi-disciplinary, top-down and bottom up approaches are important ingredients of any efforts to build long-term peace and security between Pakistan and India.
3. One of the strongest arguments for multi-track diplomacy comes from track one. There are outcomes from the civil society tracks that can support track one in its efforts to sustain

[7] Beena Sarwar, 'Women's Role in Building Peace between India and Pakistan' (Montreal: Centre for Research and Teaching on Women, McGill University, 30 July-1 August 2004), p. 13 www.mcgill.ca/mcrtw/peace/resources

the peace process and build sustainable security. One such example is the business track. The mutually beneficial relationship between the government and business track has been discussed in detail in Chapter Three. Multi-track diplomacy can also help redefine and reconfigure intractable issues, which track one is unable to do because of its position of high visibility. It can also support track one in building better channels of communication with the other side and generating inclusive and creative ideas. In the context of the ongoing 'composite dialogue', the non-governmental tracks have been responsible for widening and increasing the pace of the dialogue.[8] There have been several visits, exchanges and initiatives, which have conveyed a sense of need and desire for normalisation of relations, and this has impacted the dialogue at the track one level. Initiatives such as the visit of a 200-strong business delegation to India (organised by the Federation of Pakistan Chambers of Commerce and Industry), and the highly-publicised visits of parliamentarians to the two countries, have informed the atmosphere in which the dialogue at the track one level is taking place. Recognising that multi-track peacebuilding can propel and sustain the peace process, track one has facilitated and supported the work of the non-governmental tracks. It has done so, most importantly, by granting visas for cross-border dialogue and partnerships as well as for people requiring medical treatment. In 2003-4, there were 17 cultural delegations from India to Pakistan, and 26 delegations from Pakistan to India. There were 32 sports exchanges, and Pakistani educational institutions organised eight study tours to India. In August 2004, the Indian High Commission in Islamabad granted 7,000 visas to Pakistani citizens. Recently, through the non-governmental tracks, the Government of India facilitated a 'Made in Pakistan' fair in New Delhi. Track one has facilitated these initiatives out of a growing realisation that multi-track peacebuilding

[8] This insight was gained through private conversations with track one actors in India.

can play an important role in supporting dialogue at the track one level as well as in building the foundation for sustainable peace and security between the two countries.

4. In a context where track one engagement is deadlocked, sporadic, irregular or non-existent, as has often been the case since 1947, the need for multiple civil society tracks increases. In the past, groups such as the Women's Initiative for Peace in South Asia, Women in Security, Conflict Management and Peace and the Youth Initiative for Peace have been consistent in their peacebuilding work even when government-level interaction has been sporadic or non-existent. However, in order to avert an escalation such as the standoff in 2002, the healthy functioning of track one-and-a-half becomes extremely crucial in situations where track one communication has broken down.
5. The need for multiple tracks can also be addressed by posing the following question: What if the governments of India and Pakistan were to arrive at a political solution on the Kashmir conflict and other contentious issues? Would we still need multi-track diplomacy? The answer is yes. This is because sustainable security, as defined in this study, requires more than a political agreement on the complex issues that have sustained this conflict for more than half a century. In addition to the deeply entrenched enemy images about *the other*, there are basic human needs on both sides that need to be addressed. These include the needs of identity, security, respect and freedom from fear, to name a few. Because of the existence of these basic human needs, even if the two states were to settle all outstanding issues, multi-track processes would still have an important role to play. In this context, it is instructive to draw on conflict resolution scholar John Burton's distinction between a 'dispute' and a 'conflict'. While a dispute can be settled between states, a conflict requires that deep-seated human needs and interests be addressed if efforts for resolution are to be successful. Any settlement of the issues would, therefore, be superficial in the absence of efforts to transform the deep-rooted prejudices and suspicion that sustain this

conflict. In fact, distrust and deeply entrenched misperceptions have blocked dialogue on a range of important issues such as Kashmir and the natural gas pipeline. The transformation of conflictual relationships, institutions and mindsets (which include prejudices, beliefs, attitudes and threat perceptions) is a goal that only broad-based multi-track processes can accomplish.

6. What the majority of people in the two countries feel also conditions what the governments are able to do. Governments have a responsibility to reflect the public mood. The Indian and Pakistani governments have time and again cited the fact that they cannot push forward the peace process because public opinion in their respective countries will not allow them to do so. In this context, multi-track diplomacy is needed for two reasons. First, by transforming deeply entrenched prejudices, mistrust and misperceptions, it can build a human infrastructure in the two countries, which has the motivation and ability to advocate for, and support, sustainable notions of peace. Second, it is a very important ingredient in enabling governments to explore options and opportunities that may not be immediately visible, thereby enabling the parameters of the relationship to be changed.
7. Through its critique of realist models of security, which focus on the state and win-lose assumptions, multi-track diplomacy offers a more sustainable set of lenses through which to understand and transform conflict. It focuses on cooperation and partnerships that transcend national boundaries and foregrounds the power of relationships—human and institutional—in building long-term security. In the context of India and Pakistan, with the growing realisation that realist models are unable to provide adequate approaches for long-term security, multi-track diplomacy (without excluding the pre-eminence of governments), shifts the focus to areas such as economic cooperation, social peacebuilding and sustained civil society dialogue.
8. The need for multiple civil society tracks stems from the nature of the Indo-Pak conflict, which can be described as

protracted, deep-rooted and intractable. Emotions such as fear, suspicion, mistrust and hatred accompany and sustain such conflicts, and create antagonistic patterns of thinking. While track one acknowledges that these emotions would need to undergo significant transformation for the realisation of sustainable security, it is also acutely aware of its inability (and even the inability of track two) to address and change these patterns of thinking about *the other.* In order to transform these antagonistic patterns, the expertise of diverse multi-track actors such as social psychologists, religious leaders, trauma counsellors, dialogue facilitators and conflict resolution trainers is required. The transformation of stereotypes and prejudices are crucial if the two countries are to overcome the high levels of mistrust, hostility and mutual suspicion that sustain intractability. Multi-track diplomacy involves efforts that seek to change not only government policy, but also the way people think. Seeking to initiate radical shifts in the worldviews and basic attitudes of people, it facilitates social change by transforming diverse actors, relationships and institutions, well beyond a few leaders who sit at the negotiation table. In fact, the non-governmental tracks can complement the work of track one by addressing those areas that track one has had limited success in. These include issues relating to partition, identity and enemy images (perpetuated by socialisation processes particularly through the education system and the media), which prevent contact and deepen the process of *othering*. The non-governmental tracks have the tools, expertise and motivation to transform deep-rooted enemy images and intractable relationships between human beings and institutions in the two countries. The education track—track five—can play a particularly important role in changing the way social studies textbooks portray the other country; while the media—track nine—can also emerge as an important player if it begins to see itself as having a responsibility and a stake in the peace process.

In the context of the significant role that multi-track diplomacy can play in building sustainable security between India and Pakistan, this study makes the following recommendations:

1. Substantive interaction and collaboration between the governmental and non-governmental tracks needs to increase significantly. This includes interaction on sharing of information and analysis (communication), long-term planning and synchronisation of activities (coordination), resource sharing (cooperation), and collaboration to maximise the impact of initiatives. While there might be communication between track one and track two, there is very little information sharing among the civil society tracks and between governments and civil society. Currently, the interaction between groups such as Neemrana and the Pakistan Indian Peoples' Forum for Peace and Democracy is very limited. Even if there is some level of awareness about other initiatives, the motivation and the capacity to draw on their strengths or collaborate with them in any substantial manner, is rarely present. It is only when groups in different tracks draw on each others' strengths and link their efforts that durable peace and security will be achieved. In the absence of such coordination and collaboration, these initiatives will remain part of what has been called 'Pepsi Politics: There is a bit of fizz and then everything settles down'.[9] Having said this however, given the profound lack of contact between the two polities, several analysts believe that face-to-face communication in itself can help transform the conflict. Notes Beena Sarwar: 'No matter how limited the scope of any particular initiative, just allowing people to interact, listen, vent and learn, helps take the peace process forward by creating a lobby and a space for peace, and an atmosphere supportive of dialogue.'[10]
2. Track two diplomacy needs to significantly broaden its

[9] This metaphor was popularised by Islamabad-based political activist and development economist Kaiser Bengali.

[10] Beena Sarwar, 'Women's Role in Building Peace between India and Pakistan' (Montreal: Centre for Research and Teaching on Women, McGill University, 30 July-1 August 2004), p. 11 www.mcgill.ca/mcrtw/peace/resources

constituency by expanding the issues it addresses. Track two groups such as Neemrana should work more intensively on engaging with a broad cross-section of civil society, and enhancing civil society interaction between the two countries. This would have a profound impact on the conceptual and practical significance of track two as a concept and as a practical instrument for enhancing peace and security. Satish Kumar feels that track two should attempt to work deeper into the societies of the two countries, instead of being confined to ten people on each side of the border who meet in Islamabad and New Delhi. Engagement with a broader cross-section of society will also enable track two to communicate its ideas beyond the closed-door meetings. Further, if a constituency for peace is to be built, the socio-political structures that inform the mindsets of Indians and Pakistanis need to change. Through a broadening of their audience, track two and multi-track actors can impact these structures by helping people to realise that normalisation of bilateral relations will benefit them. The business community in the two countries presents the most potent argument in this context. This community has been able to convince large sections in the two countries that there is a dividend in having peaceful relations with *the other*—a prerequisite for economic cooperation and progress.

3. Another important area of engagement for multi-track actors needs to be with those stakeholders who might be seen as the spoilers in a peace process. It is crucial that multi-track initiatives do not remain limited to the 'peaceniks', but rather they should actively engage with those groups, which have a vested interest in perpetuating the conflict or who do not see a peace dividend emerging from the normalisation of relations.
4. Multi-track processes should build further on their ability to capture the peoples' imagination with ideas that are creative and constructive. For example, the idea of a peace park at Siachen, or the idea of a peoples' bus from Srinagar to Muzzafarabad to initiate contact between Kashmiris on both sides of the Line of Control. While the bus is not going to

> revolutionise the economy, the idea of contact for the first time in more than half a century has caught peoples' imagination. It has caught their imagination because now there is renewed hope that the future can be different from the past. Such ideas create hope in a way that technically important measures may not be able to do so.

This study concludes with a reference to Anwar al-Sadat's historic statement on 'the other walls'. The importance of multi-track processes lies in the many ways in which they can bring down the 'other walls', and facilitate new, inclusive patterns of behaviour and thinking. Such a shift is crucial if the constituency for peace is to be enlarged and an environment conducive for dialogue is to be built. Officially brokered peace agreements represent only part of the solution to the conflict between Pakistan and India. Equally important is a focus on changing the average Indian/Pakistani's pattern of thinking about *the other*. No political agreement at the state level can act as a substitute for this process of humanisation and relationship building. By empowering people from all walks of life to take ownership of the peace process, multi-track diplomacy can play a crucial role in facilitating what Harold Saunders calls a 'public peace process'. The hope today, for Pakistan and India, is that more and more citizens, representing different generations and diverse professional backgrounds, will traverse these tracks.

CHAPTER SIX

Conclusion
From Intractability to Sustainability

> The real voyage of discovery consists not in seeking new landscapes but in having new eyes.
>
> MARCEL PROUST

The research for this study began with the question: How can social change processes be initiated and sustained between Pakistan and India?

This study introduced the conceptual framework of multi-track diplomacy as a road map for achieving sustainable peace and security. It argued that the mere absence of social and political conflict does not ensure peace and security. For any formulation of security to be sustainable, it has to be perceived as being *just* and mutually enhancing. It needs to be able to guarantee certain minimum assurances (for instance, freedom from fear and discrimination) to broad sections of civil society and provide a space for communities and individuals to articulate their own aspirations and participate in decision-making about security issues. This would mean arriving at a broad consensus amongst competing actors about how such a formulation of security might be achieved.

This is where multi-track diplomacy can play an important role through its focus on diverse strategies (face-to-face dialogues, conflict resolution trainings, coexistence camps, media engagement, etc.), actors (grassroots groups, government diplomats, media, business leaders, women's groups, private citizens, NGOs, etc.) and approaches to peacebuilding (some that address the immediate issues of contention, and others that address the more long-term issues relating to systemic and institutional change and the rebuilding of human relationships).

This study advocates a need to focus on those who John Paul Lederach defines as the 'strategic who'—a diverse group of actors who can initiate sustainable social change by pooling in their skills, energies and resources. The 'strategic who', explains Lederach, are those actors who through 'their actions have the capacity to replicate and exponentially affect the larger whole'.[1] These actors represent vocations not conventionally associated with the field of peace-building, but who nevertheless have the ability to significantly impact the peace process between the two countries. In addition to government diplomats, politicians and conflict resolution professionals, these actors include the business community, the media, grant-making organisations, private citizens, activists, religious leaders, educational institutions and women's movements.

Another unique feature of the multi-track framework is its focus on building capacity. Capacity includes motivation, attitude and skill. In the preceding pages, this study has introduced a range of approaches through which the capacity to build sustainable security between Pakistan and India can be generated. Another important attribute is the depth of a peace process. The concept of depth points to the need for processes of humanisation, which can transform 'enemy images' of perceived others. The transformation of stereotypes and prejudices, about communities and nations, are crucial if countries such as India and Pakistan are to overcome the high levels of mistrust, hostility and mutual suspicion that sustain intractability. The framework of multi-track diplomacy facilitates such depth when diverse actors, relationships and institutions, well beyond the few political leaders who sit at the negotiation table, are transformed.

The vision of sustainable security invites governments and civil societies to develop an awareness of the complex, underlying dynamics of deep-rooted protracted conflicts and to build the capacity to transform such situations into collaborative processes

[1] John Paul Lederach, 'Building Mediative Capacity in Deep Rooted Conflict', *The Fletcher Forum of World Affairs*, Vol. 26: 1 (Winter/Spring 2002), pp. 91-101.

of conflict resolution and peacebuilding. In addition, it draws attention to the need for an environment where the peace dividend is so high that parties to a conflict would want to invest resources in the peace process, and would, therefore, see weaponisation programmes as being detrimental to the long-term goal of security. Such a formulation of security also suggests a need to redefine power—from 'power over' to 'power with'. This kind of power is derived from a focus on common interests rather than on gaining an edge in bargaining over conflicting interests. This in turn entails the formation of partnerships and the participation of multiple sectors for a common purpose.

LOOKING AHEAD

During the course of this research, interviews were conducted (between March and July 2004) with a broad cross-section of women and men from Pakistan and India. While a majority agreed that the recent resumption of track one dialogue could in part be attributed to pressure from civil society, it was felt that several domestic and international compulsions, the 'war on terrorism' in particular, were also responsible for pushing the two governments to the dialogue table. The reasons, therefore, for the ongoing dialogue were seen as being more tactical than strategic.

This, in turn, suggests that once these international factors are no longer compelling, the two governments might not feel an overwhelming need to sustain the peace process. It is in this context that multi-track diplomacy gains significance as a process through which the political environment and general public opinion can be transformed, and strategic constituencies for peace can emerge and provide an enduring foundation for sustainable security.

In the context of India and Pakistan, progress on the Kashmir issue ('the unfinished business of partition') and 'cross-border terrorism' would be among the important elements of any sustainable security formulation. In addition, some other elements that would need to be addressed include Siachen, nuclear risk reduction and economic relations (for instance, the Iran-Pakistan-India gas pipeline, which could transform bilateral cooperation).

However, in addition to these, there are a range of issues that sustain the conflict and that track one is ill equipped to transform. These include issues relating to partition, identity and enemy images (perpetuated by socialisation processes particularly through the education system and the media). The education track—track five—can play a particularly important role in changing the way social studies' textbooks portray the other country; while the mass media—track nine—can also emerge as an important player if it begins to see itself as having a responsibility and a stake in the peace process.

In this context, it is highly debatable that a political resolution of the Kashmir conflict would build sustainable peace and security. In addition to Kashmir, there is the poisonous relationship between the two countries. The interviews conducted with Indians and Pakistanis during the course of this research point to the important role that socially constructed enemy images have played in sustaining this conflict. While track one can sign a political agreement on Kashmir, it cannot transform the stereotypes and prejudices that lie at the root of the hostility. The transformation of conflictual human relationships (which include beliefs, attitudes and threat perceptions) is a goal that only citizens outside government can accomplish.[2]

Cross-border multi-track initiatives involving different sections of society have the ability to facilitate a much needed humanisation of perceived *others*, counter the hate propaganda about the other country, and most importantly, *conscientise* the next generation of opinion-shapers that a different future is possible.[3] They can also develop a web of relationships: between individuals, communities, organisations, businesses, governments, and cultural, religious, political and economic institutions and movements. Such a web of

[2] In many of the interviews conducted with Pakistanis and Indians, the image of the 'Hindu expansionist state', which has not accepted the existence of Pakistan and the image of an 'Islamic terrorist state', which threatens the territorial integrity of India, emerged as important components of the socialisation process that citizens in the two countries have undergone

[3] Rizwan Zeb, Research Analyst with the Institute of Regional Studies, Islamabad, adds an important caveat to this. He feels that multi-track efforts need to engage with the perceptions of people in each country before they can begin to address cross-border perceptions. An email interview with Rizwan Zeb was conducted in July 2004.

relationships is crucial if peace and security are to be sustainable. 'Relationships are a form of power or social capital. By connecting people, relationships form an architecture of peacebuilding networks that allow people to cooperate and coordinate to constructively address and prevent violent conflict.'[4] This suggests that sustainable security requires the building of relationships between civil societies, not just between states.

Recognising the need for such relationships, former Israeli Prime Minister, Golda Meir, speaking in the context of the peace process between Israel and Egypt, had once said: 'When Israelis shop in the markets of Cairo, I will know that there is real peace and security.' In the context of India and Pakistan, how would we recognise social change if we saw it? Would the presence of thousands of Indians in Pakistan—in the markets, in the cricket stadiums, and in the homes of Pakistanis—enjoying the overwhelming hospitality, friendship and warmth of their hosts, be an indicator of social change? If so, one can say in no uncertain terms that social change has begun.

[4] Lisa Schirch and Manjrika Sewak, 'The Role of Women in Peacebuilding', Issue Paper Commissioned by the European Centre for Conflict Prevention in 2004 (www.gppac.net), pp. 4-5.

Select Bibliography

Ahmar, Moonis (ed.), *Internal and External Dynamics of South Asian Security* (Karachi: Fazeelsons, 2001).

Ahmar, Moonis and Farhan Hanif Siddiqi (ed.), *The Challenges of Conflict Resolution and Security in the 21st Century: Problems and Prospects* (Karachi: Karachi University Press, 2001).

Anderson, Gillian (ed.), *Women and Peace: A Practical Resource Pack* (London: International Alert, 2000).

Bajpai, Kanti, 'Human Security: Concept and Measurement', *Kroc Institute Occasional Paper #19: OP: 1* (Notre Dame, Indiana: The Joan B. Kroc Institute for International Peace Studies, August 2000).

Banerji, Dipankar (ed.), *Confidence Building Measures in South Asia* (Colombo: RCSS, 1999).

Basrur, Rajesh (ed.), *Security in the New Millennium: Views from South Asia* (New Delhi: India Research Press, 2001).

Behera, Navnita Chadha, 'Forging New Solidarities: Non-official Dialogues', in Monique Mekenkamp, Paul Van Tongeren and Hans van de Veen (eds), *Searching for Peace in Central and South Asia* (Boulder: Lynne Rienner Publishers, 2003).

Behera, Navnita Chadha, Paul M. Evans and Gowher Rizvi, *Beyond Boundaries: A Report on the State of Non-Official Dialogues on Peace, Security and Co-operation in South Asia* (Ontario: University of Toronto/York University, 1997).

Behera, Navnita Chadha, Victor Gunawardena, Shahid Kardar and Raisul Awal Mahmood, *People-to-People Contact in South Asia* (New Delhi: Manohar, 2000).

Boulding, Elise, 'The Challenges of Imaging Peace in Wartime', in *Futures*, Vol. 23, No. 5 (1991).

Boulding, Kenneth, *Stable Peace* (Austin: University of Texas Press, 1978).

Burton, John, *Conflict: Human Needs Theory* (Wellington: Macmillan Press Ltd, 1993).

Butalia, Urvashi, *The Other Side of Silence: Voices from the Partition of India* (New Delhi: Penguin Books, 1998).

Buzan, Barry, Ole Waever and Jaap de Wilde, *Security: A New Framework for Analysis* (Boulder: Lynne Rienner Publishers, 1998).

Chhachhi, Amrita, 'Of Knots and Weaves: Indian and Pakistani Women Connect across Borders', *South Asia Citizens' Web* www.sacw.net/i_aii/pag_a.html (August 1996).

Clements, Kevin, 'Civil Society and Conflict Prevention', *Facing Ethnic Conflicts* (Bonn: Centre for Development Research, 14-16 December 2000).

Curle, Adam, *Tools for Transformation: A Personal Study* (Stroud: Hawthorn Press, 1990).

Davies, John and Edward Kaufman, *Second Track/Citizen's Diplomacy: Concepts and Techniques for Conflict Transformation* (Maryland: Rowman and Littlefield, 2003).

Diamond, Louise and John McDonald, *Multi-Track Diplomacy: A Systems Approach to Peace,* 3rd edn. (West Hartford, Connecticut: Kumarian Press, 1996).

Durrani, Mahmud Ali, *India and Pakistan: The Cost of Conflict and the Benefits of Peace* (Karachi: Oxford University Press, 2001).

Fisher, Simon, et al., *Working with Conflict: Skills and Strategies for Action* (London: Zed Books in association with Responding to Conflict, 2000).

Galtung, Johan, *Peace by Peaceful Means: Peace and Conflict, Development and Civilization* (Thousand Oaks: Sage, 1996).

Gopinath, Meenakshi and Manjrika Sewak, *Transcending Conflict: A Resource Book on Conflict Transformation* (New Delhi: WISCOMP, 2003).

Haq, Mahbub ul, 'New Imperatives of Human Security', *RGICS Paper No. 17* (New Delhi: Rajiv Gandhi Foundation, 1994).

Howard, Ross, Francis Rolt, Hans van de Veen and Juliette Verhoeven (eds), *The Power of the Media: A Handbook for Peacebuilders* (Utrecht: European Centre for Conflict Prevention in cooperation with the European Centre for Common Ground and IMPACS, 2003).

Kelman, Herbert, 'Interactive Problem-Solving: A Social-Psychological Approach to Conflict Resolution', in W. Klassen (ed.), *Dialogue toward Inter-Faith Understanding* (Jerusalem: Ecumenical Institute for Theological Research, 1986).

Khagram, Sanjeev, William Clark and Dana Firas Raad, 'From the Environment and Human Security to Sustainable Security and

Development', in *Journal of Human Development,* Vol. 4, No. 2 (Cambridge, MA: Carfax Publishing, July 2003).

Lederach, John Paul, 'Building Mediative Capacity in Deep Rooted Conflict', *The Fletcher Forum of World Affairs,* Vol. 26: 1 (Winter/ Spring 2002).

———, *Building Peace: Sustainable Reconciliation in Divided Societies* (Washington DC: United States Institute of Peace Press, 1997).

———, *Preparing for Peace: Conflict Transformation across Cultures* (New York: Syracuse University Press, 1996).

Lorentzen, Lois and Jennifer Turpin (eds), *The Women and War Reader* (New York: New York University Press, 1998).

Manchanda, Rita, 'Redefining and Feminizing Security', *Economic and Political Weekly*, Vol. 36, No. 22 (Mumbai, 2 June 2001).

McDonald, John and James Notter, 'Track Two Diplomacy: Non-governmental Strategies for Peace', *U.S. Foreign Policy Agenda* (Washington DC: USIA, December 1996).

McDonald, John, 'The Need for Multi-Track Diplomacy', *Occasional Paper Number 9* (Washington DC: The Institute for Multi-Track Diplomacy, May 2000).

Menon, Ritu and Kamla Bhasin, *Borders and Boundaries: Women in India's Partition* (New Delhi: Kali for Women, 2000).

Moser, Caroline O.N. and Fiona C. Clark (eds), *Victims, Perpetrators or Actors? Gender, Armed Conflict and Political Violence* (New Delhi: Kali for Women, 2001).

Pankhurst, Donna, *Mainstreaming Gender: A Framework for Action* (London: International Alert, 1999).

Reardon, Betty, 'Women or Weapons: The Militarist Sexist Symbiosis', in Ingeborg Breines et al. (eds), *Towards a Women's Agenda for a Culture of Peace* (Paris: UNESCO Publishing, 1999).

Reychler, Luc and Thania Paffenholz (eds.), *Peacebuilding: A Field Guide* (Boulder: Lynne Rienner Publishers, 2001).

Rothman, Jay, *Resolving Identity-based Conflict in Nations, Organisations and Communities* (San Francisco: Jossey-Bass Publishers, 1997).

Sarwar, Beena, 'Women's Role in Building Peace between India and Pakistan' (Montreal: Centre for Research and Teaching on Women, McGill University, 30 July-1 August 2004) www.mcgill.ca/mcrtw/ peace/resources.

Saunders, Harold H., *A Public Peace Process: Sustained Dialogue to Transform Racial and Ethnic Conflicts* (New York: Palgrave, 2001).

———, *The Other Walls: The Arab-Israeli Peace Process in a Global Perspective*, rev. edn. (Princeton: Princeton University, 1991).

———, 'When Citizens Talk', *Kettering Review* (Washington DC: Summer 1984).

Schukoske, Jane and Manjrika Sewak, 'Track Five Diplomacy: Roles for Higher Educational Institutions in Conflict Transformation', in Mizanur Rahman (ed.), *Human Rights and Globalisation* (Dhaka: Empowerment through Law of the Common People, December 2003).

Shuman, Michael, Gale Warner and Lila Forest, 'Citizen Diplomacy', *In Context Quarterly* (Washington DC: Context Institute, Winter 1987).

Tickner, J. Ann, *Gender in International Relations: Feminist Perspectives on Achieving Global Security* (New York: Columbia University Press, 1992).

Tongeren, Paul van, Malin Brenk, Marte Hellema and Juliette Verhoeven (eds), *People Building Peace II: Successful Stories of Civil Society* (Boulder: Lynne Rienner Publishers, 2005).

Voorhees, James, *Dialogue Sustained: The Multilevel Peace Process and the Dartmouth Conference* (Washington DC: United States Institute of Peace Press and Charles Kettering Foundation, 2002).

Waslekar, Sundeep, 'Track Two Diplomacy in South Asia', *ACDIS Occasional Paper: Research of the Program in Arms Control, Disarmament and International Security* (Urbana-Champaign: University of Illinois, October 1995).

RCSS PUBLICATIONS

- *Defence, Technology and Cooperative Security in South Asia: Report on the Proceedings of the Tenth Summer Workshop* (RCSS, 2004)
- *Environment Development and Human Security: Perspectives from South Asia* (2003)
- *Terrorism in South Asia: Impact on Development and Democratic Process* (SIPRA, 2003)
- *South Asia and the War on Terrorism* (India Research Press, 2003)
- *Shaping the Future–A South Asian Civil Society Dialogue* (RCSS, July 2002)
- *Small Arms and Human Insecurity* (RCSS, July 2002)
- *SAARC in the Twenty-First Century: Towards a Cooperative Future* (July 2002)
- *Memories of a Genocidal Partition: The Haunting Tale of Victims, Witnesses and Perpetrators* (RCSS, July 2002)
- *South Asian Security Futures: A Dialogue of Director's Regional Strategic Studies Institutes* (March 2002)
- *Security and Governance in South Asia* (September 2001)
- *Globalization and Non-Traditional Security in South Asia* (September 2001)
- *Security in the New Millennium* (India Research Press, 2001)
- *The Simla Agreement 1972: Its Wasted Promise* (Manohar, 2001)

RCSS Newsletter

A quarterly bulletin, it publishes a brief report of RCSS activities, presentations at its workshops on topics of contemporary interest and news and programmes of the RCSS and its alumnae.

RCSS Policy Studies

33 Small Arms and the Security Debate in South Asia (Manohar, 2005)

32 New Nuclear Triangle and China's Role in South Asia (forthcoming)

31 Stability through Economic Cooperation in a Nuclear Environment (Manohar, 2005)

29 The Role of Mediation in Resolving India-Pakistan Conflict: Parameters and Possibilities (Manohar, 2005)

28 HIV/AIDS as a Security Threat to India (Manohar, 2005)

27 Nepal's Maoist Movement and Implications for India and China (Manohar, 2005)

26 Elite Perceptions in Foreign Policy: Role of Print Media in Influencing India-Pakistan Relations, 1989-1999 (Manohar, 2004)

Nuclear Risk Reduction Measures and Restraint Regime in South Asia (Manohar, 2004)

24 River Water Sharing Problem Between India and Pakistan: Case Study of the Indus Basin Water Treaty (June 2004)

23 Christianity and Political Conflict in India: The Case of Gujarat (June 2002)

Fellowship in South Asian Alternatives (FISAA) Monograph

- Water, Power and People: A South Asian Manifesto on the Politics and Knowledge of Water (1997)
- The Nuclear Debate: Ironies and Immoralities (1998)

Others

- *Directory of Individuals and Institutions Engaged in South Asian Strategic Studies* (1998).